CALIFORNIA
DMV HANDBOOK 2024

DRIVER LICENSE

ID: 123-456-789-10

DOB: DD/MM/YYYY   ISS: DD/MM/YYYY

EXP: DD/MM/YYYY

NAME SURNAME

CLASS:

SEX   WGT

HGT   EYES

YOUR COMPLETE GUIDE TO DRIVER'S LICENSE EXAM
PREPARATION AND SAFE DRIVING PRACTICES WITH
300+ QUESTIONS AND ANSWERS

STEVEN J. WILKINS

TABLE OF CONTENT

INTRODUCTION

Welcome to the California DMV Handbook 2024, your go-to guide for mastering the ins and outs of driving in the Golden State. Dive into a journey through the diverse landscapes of California's roadways, where each page unfolds like a scenic vista, revealing the secrets to confident and responsible driving.

Buckle up for a ride through traffic signs, road etiquette, and the unique driving culture of California. Picture yourself seamlessly merging into lanes of wisdom, navigating intersections with finesse, and decoding the language of traffic signs on this captivating odyssey.

This isn't just a guide; it's an engaging experience designed to transform you into a discerning and informed driver. Engage with captivating stories, insightful tips, and practical strategies that elevate your understanding of the road.

As you turn each page, anticipate a roadmap to success – not just in passing the DMV test but in becoming a vigilant and adept driver in California. The California DMV Handbook 2024 is more than a handbook; it's a narrative that draws you into the captivating world of responsible driving.

Are you ready to start this transformative journey? The California DMV Handbook 2024 awaits your indispensable companion for unlocking the artistry of driving through the sun-soaked highways and coastal curves of the Golden State. Let the adventure begin!

About The Author

Greetings! I'm Steven J. Wilkins, your go-to guide for unraveling the complexities of California's driving rules. Having successfully navigated the DMV test on my first try, I bring practical insights to your journey.

Imagine a determined individual armed with the California DMV handbook and a passion for mastering driving. As the author, I delved into the handbook, revealing the keys to success through strategic study sessions and practical scenarios.

Tips for success? Prioritize understanding, involve yourself in real-life scenarios, and embrace interactive learning tools. I aim to empower you with the strategies that led to my triumph. Join me on this road where expertise meets experience, making success not just a destination but a journey.

Facts About This Handbook

1. Get the latest info on California's driving laws in 2024 with this handbook.

2. Road rules, traffic signals, and updates dive into a complete guide to California's driving scene.

3.Explore practical scenarios and real-life examples to apply your knowledge to everyday driving.

4.Quizzes, practice tests, and visuals make learning engaging and effective.

5.Navigate through the material effortlessly with a logical and user-friendly structure.

6.Visual aids like diagrams ensure a visually appealing approach to understanding complex driving concepts.

7.Find valuable tips and strategies throughout to boost your confidence for the DMV exam.

8. Aligned with California DMV standards, ensuring accuracy for your official exam.

9. Overcome common study hurdles with practical solutions provided in the handbook.

10.Prepare not just for the test but for real-world driving in California, promoting safe and informed habits on the roads.

How To Use This Handbook

Maximize your use of the California DMV handbook for 2024 with these effective steps:

1. Get familiar with the handbook's structure. Know how it's organized into sections.

2. Take your time reading. Absorb key info on road rules, traffic signals, and driving laws.

3. Jot down important points and regulations as you read to reinforce your understanding.

4. Engage with quizzes and practice tests. This interactive approach reinforces knowledge.

5. Focus on practical scenarios. See how theory applies to real driving situations.

6. Use diagrams and illustrations to simplify complex concepts.

7. Look for tips on tackling common challenges faced by test-takers.

8. Manage study sessions effectively to avoid feeling overwhelmed.

9. Consistency is key. Revisit challenging sections regularly for reinforcement.

10. Relate handbook content to real-world driving experiences for practical understanding.

11.Keep an eye out for handbook updates and stay informed on the latest driving laws in California.

Success on the DMV exam comes from understanding, regular practice, and applying knowledge to real scenarios. Let the handbook be your guide, ensuring you're well-prepared for a successful driving journey in California.

Dmv Exam Tips

- Kick off your exam prep with ample time for thorough review.
- Understand, don't just memorize the driving rules. Apply this knowledge in real-world scenarios.
- Reinforce understanding with regular quizzes, getting familiar with the exam format.
- Focus on sections where you struggle to ensure a balanced knowledge base.
- Engage with interactive tools for a more effective and engaging study experience.
- Practice under conditions similar to the actual exam to familiarize yourself with the testing environment.
- Analyze practice exam mistakes, understand why, and take corrective measures.
- Use diagrams and illustrations for better memory retention.
- Practice relaxation techniques for a calm mindset on exam day.
- Pay close attention to question-wording to avoid misinterpretation.
- Don't leave any questions unanswered. Make an educated guess if needed.
- Use your exam time wisely; pace yourself to answer all questions.
- Be aware of recent updates in driving laws; stay informed about the latest regulations.
- On exam day, briefly revisit key points from the handbook.
- Ensure you have all required identification and documentation as per DMV's specifications.

Chapter 1: Getting Ready for Your Driver's License

Understanding the California DMV

The California DMV is your key to mastering driving, holding crucial knowledge for every driver. It's not just about passing a test; it's about embracing the responsibility that comes with driving in this dynamic state.

Within the DMV's pages lies a tapestry of regulations ensuring road safety. It's a language of signs painting a portrait of responsible driving on California's highways. Understanding the DMV goes beyond the handbook; it's recognizing the heartbeat of a state pulsing through its roads. It's a driving companion, offering insights into California's unique driving culture, empowering every driver.

Consider the DMV a guide through licensing complexities, demystifying bureaucracy into a comprehensible roadmap for drivers at every stage.

Knowledge from the DMV isn't just a requirement; it's power. It enables informed decisions, and safeguards, and contributes to a culture of responsible driving.

What sets apart understanding the California DMV is its tailor-made relevance to the state's diverse driving landscape. It's embracing a way of life connected to the state's identity.
The DMV isn't a hurdle; it's a prelude to driving freedom, an investment in a future where every driver fosters a safe environment.

More than bureaucracy, the California DMV is a reservoir of knowledge, a cultural touchstone, guiding through the evolving landscape of California driving. Understanding it is an initiation into a community of responsible drivers, contributing to the shared narrative of the road. Welcome to the journey of understanding the California DMV, where knowledge becomes the compass for a seamless driving experience in the Golden State.

Obtaining Your Learner's Permit

Before you begin, check if you meet California's eligibility criteria – at least 15 and a half years old and enrolled in an approved driver's education program.

Select a DMV-approved driver's education course, either online or in a classroom. Cover key topics like road rules and safe driving practices.

Get Form DL44 from the DMV website or a local office, and complete it with a parent or guardian's signature, affirming their consent.

Gather necessary documents, including proof of identity, social security number, and residency. The DMV website has a full list of acceptable documents.

Schedule a permit test online or by calling the DMV. Recent changes allow most services, including scheduling, to be done online.

Study the California Driver Handbook thoroughly to prepare for the written test. Know the latest laws, road signs, and driving regulations.

Show up at the DMV for your appointment, ready for the written test. Pass to move forward in the process.

Upon passing, get a learner's permit, allowing you to practice driving under specific conditions.

Maximize your permit by completing at least 50 hours of supervised driving, including 10 hours at night.

Consider a behind-the-wheel training course for structured driving instruction, enhancing your preparation.

Once you're confident after meeting practice hours, schedule the driving test with the DMV.

Pass the driving test to get your provisional license, a significant step toward full licensure.

With your provisional license, keep honing your skills and practicing safe driving. Responsible driving is a lifelong commitment.

Follow these steps, stay informed with the latest DMV procedures, and pave the way for a successful journey from a learner's permit to full driving independence. Safe travels on your path to becoming a licensed driver in California!

Studying For The Written Exam Deep

Prepare for the exam by starting your study routine well in advance. Opt for shorter, regular study sessions to enhance retention and focus.

Understand the exam structure, including question count, time limits, and scoring. Tailor your study plan accordingly.

Thoroughly read the handbook, emphasizing road rules, traffic signs, and essential regulations. Take notes to reinforce understanding.

Use online resources and apps for interactive learning, such as practice quizzes, to make studying engaging and effective.

Identify weak areas through practice tests and focus on balancing your knowledge foundation.

Summarize key information on flashcards for quick periodic reviews, reinforcing memory.

Practice with official sample tests provided by the DMV to familiarize yourself with the exam format.

Take practice tests under exam-like conditions to simulate the actual testing environment.

Join study groups or review sessions with peers to deepen understanding through discussion.

Regularly check for updates to California driving laws to stay informed with the latest information.

Relate theoretical knowledge to real-world scenarios, understanding how handbook rules apply to everyday driving.

Avoid cramming, take breaks during study sessions, and manage stress to maintain focus.

Thoroughly review mistakes after practice tests to understand correct answers and avoid similar errors.

Utilize visual aids, diagrams, and mnemonics to memorize complex information, enhancing recall.

Maintain a positive mindset throughout your study journey; confidence is crucial for success.

Combine these strategies with consistent effort, and you'll be well-prepared for the California DMV written exam.

300+ Practice Tests and Answers

Practice Tests 1

1.. What does this sign below mean?

A: A flagger is in charge of the traffic up front.
B:Children crossing the street ahead
C:Crossing the school zone ahead

Correct Answer is Option A: A flagger is in charge of the traffic up front

2. This warning sign indicate:

A: You are approaching a four-way intersection;
B: You are approaching a railroad crossing;
C: You are entering a restricted zone.

Correct Answer is Option B: You are approaching a railroad crossing;

3. This sign, which is red and white, indicates that:

A: You have the right-of-way;
B: Give way to oncoming traffic;
C: Vehicles on the right move first.

Correct Answer is Option B: Give way to oncoming traffic

4. This sign indicates:

A: Pedestrians strolling along the road ahead

B: Pedestrian crossing ahead

C: Do not cross here

Correct Answer is Option B: Pedestrian crossing ahead

5. The following sign indicates:

A: Beware of large vehicles ahead.

B: A steep hill ahead.

C: Warning sign for the drawbridge ahead

Correct Answer is Option B: Steep Hill ahead

6. This red and white regulatory sign means:

A: No left turn can be made here

B: A left turn can be made only after stopping

C: All traffic must turn right at the next intersection

Correct Answer is Option A: No left turn can be made here

7. This road sign means:

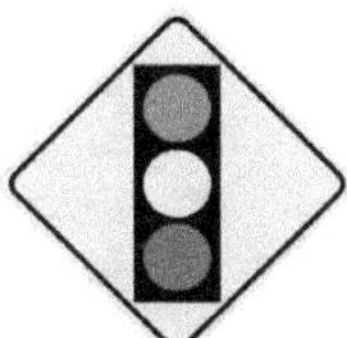

A: Be prepared to stop if the light is flashing
B: There is a traffic signal ahead
C: Controlled railroad ahead

Correct Answer is Option B: There is a traffic signal ahead

8. What does the below red and white sign indicate?

A: The road ahead is closed to traffic in all directions
B: Yield the right of way
C: The road is closed to traffic in your direction

Correct Answer is Option C: The road is closed to traffic in your direction

9. This warning sign means:

A: Road is Slippery When Wet
B: Winding road ahead
C: Road with sharp turns ahead

Correct Answer is Option A: Road is Slippery When Wet

10. This five-sided sign indicates:

A: You are approaching pedestrian Crossing

B: You are near a school

C: The road ahead is a walking trail

Correct Answer is Option B: You are near a school

11. The below sign indicates:

A: Merging traffic entering from the left

B: Warning left lane ends ahead

C: Warning one-way road ahead

Correct Answer is Option A: Merging traffic entering from the left

12. This warning sign means:

A: Winding road ahead begins with a curve to the left

B: Passing allowed from left and right

C: Winding road ahead begins with a curve to the right

Correct Answer is Option C: Winding road ahead begins with a curve to the right

13. What does the below sign mean?

A: Divided highway ends
B: Keep to the right of obstruction
C: Left lane ends

Correct Answer is Option B: Keep to the right of obstruction

14. This sign means:

A: Intersection warning ahead, roadway ends must turn right or left
B: Side Road intersection ahead
C: Y intersection ahead

Correct Answer is Option A: Intersection warning ahead, roadway ends must turn right or left

15. When you see this sign at an intersection, you must:

A: Stop only if you see pedestrians crossing
B: Slow down and yield to oncoming traffic
C: Come to a complete stop, proceed only when safe to do so

Correct Answer is Option C: Come to a complete stop, proceed only when safe to do so

16. This exit speed advisory sign means:

A: Slow down, maximum advised speed is 25 miles per hour in ideal conditions

B: Slow down, maximum advised speed is 25 miles per hour in all conditions

C: Minimum advised speed limit is 25 miles per hour in all conditions**Correct Answer is**

Option A: Slow down, maximum advised speed is 25 miles per hour in ideal conditions

17. What does the below sign indicate?

A: Warning divided highway ends ahead

B: Winding Road advance notice

C: Two-way traffic advance warning

Correct Answeri is Option A: Warning divided highway ends ahead

18. This below sign means:

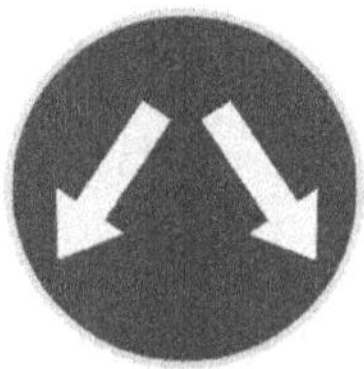

A: Traffic is permitted to pass on either side of an island or obstruction

B: Right lane stays to the right, left lane stays to the left

C: Keep to the left, merging traffic ahead

Correct Answer is Option A: Traffic is permitted to pass on either side of an island or obstruction

19. This sign at an intersection means:

A: No right turn permitted at this intersection
B: No right turn on red light
C: All traffic must turn left at the next intersection

Correct Answer is Option A: No right turn permitted at this intersection

20. This sign means there is.

A: Wildlife Reserve ahead
B: Deer crossing ahead
C: Zoo nearby

Correct Answer is Option B: Deer crossing ahead

21. This sign means.

A: Right lane ends, merge left
B: Road narrows ahead
C: Passing is allowed on the right lane

Correct Answer is Option A: Right lane ends, merge left

22. This regulatory sign means.

A: Passing is not permitted in this zone
B: You may not park at locations where this sign is installed
C: Pedestrian crossing is prohibited

Correct Answer is   Option B: You may not park at locations where this sign is installed

23. On a three-lane highway, this sign means.

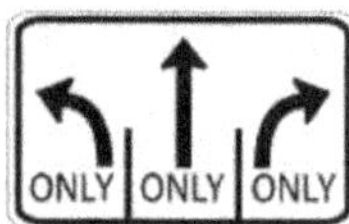

A: All lanes permit left and right turns
B: Left lane must turn left, center lane must go straight, right lane must turn right
C: Center lane permits you to go straight, left, or right

Correct Answer is Option B: Left lane must turn left, center lane must go straight, right lane must turn Right

24. This sign on a center lane means you may use this lane for.

A: Turning left or right only
B: Passing slow-moving vehicles only
C: Turning left only

Correct Answer is Option C: Turning left only

25. This sign means.

A: New lane will be added to the left in the same direction, merging not required
B: Left lane ends and merges to the right
C: Passing on the left permitted ahead

Correct Answer is Option A: New lane will be added to the left in the same direction, merging not required

26. At an intersection, this sign means.

A: Before making a U-turn, you must come to a complete stop
B: No U-turns are permitted at this intersection
C: You must yield to all other oncoming traffic before turning

Correct Answer is Option B: No U-turns are permitted at this intersection

27. This warning sign indicates.

A: You will encounter a railroad crossing when turning right at the intersection ahead
B: You will encounter a railroad crossing when turning left at the intersection ahead
C: Railroad crossing straight ahead

Correct Answer is Option A: You will encounter a railroad crossing when turning right at the intersection ahead

28. This traffic sign tells you.

A: The road you are traveling on intersects a highway ahead

B: The main road curves to the left with a side road entering from the right

C: There is a three-way intersection up ahead on the road

Correct Answer is Option C: There is a three-way intersection up ahead on the road

29. What does the below sign indicate?

A: This road crosses a narrow bridge ahead

B: Soft shoulder warning ahead

C: Railway tracks ahead

Correct Answer is Option A: This road crosses a narrow bridge ahead

30. This road sign means.

A: Sharp right turn ahead

B: A road joins from the right

C: The road ahead turns sharply right then sharply left

Correct Answer is Option C: The road ahead turns sharply right then sharply left

31 When you see a bicyclist on the road ahead with their left arm extended downward to their left, you should assume the bicyclist is:

A: Signaling that they are slowing down or stopping.

B: Signaling to change lanes to the left or make a left turn.

C: Just stretching their arm; it is not a signal of anything.

Correct Answer: A: Signaling that they are slowing down or stopping.

32. When you are driving on a highway that does not have a paved shoulder, if your vehicle breaks down, you should:

A: Try to get your vehicle completely out of the traffic lanes and off the paved surface of the highway before stopping.

B: Try to bring your vehicle to a stop on the right side of the highway with all four wheels still on the paved surface.

C: Try to stop your vehicle with your right wheels off the paved surface of the highway and your left wheels still on the paved surface.

Correct Answer: A: Try to get your vehicle completely out of the traffic lanes and off the paved surface of the highway before stopping.

33. If you are the driver or owner of a vehicle in a crash that is your fault and you are not insured in compliance with the financial responsibility law:

A: You will be placed on probation for up to 4 months.

B: You must attend a driver financial responsibility course.

C: Before your driving privileges are restored, you could have to pay for the damages.

Correct Answer: C: Before your driving privileges are restored, you could have to pay for the damages.

34. If you are a licensed driver under the age of 17, you must be accompanied by a driver who is 21 years of age or older and holds a valid Class E or higher driver license if you want to operate a motor vehicle between:

A: 10:00 p.m. and 6:00 a.m. unless you are driving to or from work.

B: 11:00 p.m. and 6:00 a.m. unless you are driving to or from work.

C: Midnight and 7:00 a.m. unless you are driving to or from work.

Correct Answer: B: 11:00 p.m. and 6:00 a.m. unless you are driving to or from work.

Practice Tests 2

1. When passing another vehicle off the paved roadway, you should only do so:
   A) If the shoulder can accommodate your vehicle
   B) If the car in front is making a left turn
   C) Under no circumstances

Correct answer: C) Under no circumstances

2. Approaching a railroad crossing with limited visibility, the speed limit is:
   A) 15 miles per hour
   B) 20 miles per hour
   C) 25 miles per hour

Correct answer: A) 15 miles per hour

3. When parallel parking on a level street, your wheels must be within:
   A) 18 inches of the curb
   B) Turned toward the street
   C) One of your rear wheels touching the curb

Correct answer: A) 18 inches of the curb

4. While merging onto the freeway, you should be driving:
   A) At or near the same speed as freeway traffic
   B) 5 to 10 mph less quickly than on a freeway
   C) The posted speed limit for the freeway

Correct answer: A) At or near the same speed as freeway traffic

5. In foggy conditions, use your:
   A) Fog lights only
   B) High beams
   C) Low beams

Correct answer: C) Low beams

6. A white painted curb indicates a loading zone for:
   A) Freight or passengers
   B) Passengers or mail only
   C) Freight only

Correct answer: B) Passengers or mail only

7. When a school bus is stopped with red lights flashing, you should:
   A) Stop and proceed when children exit
   B) Reduce to 25 mph and move carefully through.
   C) As long as the red lights remain flashing, stop

Correct answer: C) As long as the red lights remain flashing, stop

8. California's basic speed law states:
   A) Never drive faster than posted limits
   B) Never drive faster than safe conditions
   C) Max speed limit in California is 70 mph on certain freeways

Correct answer: B) Never drive faster than safe conditions

9. After selling your vehicle, notify the DMV within:
   A) 5 days
   B) 10 days
   C) 15 days

Correct answer: A) 5 days

10. To avoid last-minute moves, look down the road about:
   A) 5 to 10 seconds
   B) 10 to 15 seconds
   C) 15 to 20 seconds

Correct answer: B) 10 to 15 seconds

11. When preparing for a left turn, signal continuously for:

A: 50 feet
B: 75 feet
C: 100 feet

Correct Answer: C: 100 feet

12. What's true about blind spots?
 A: Eliminated with mirrors on each side
 B: Larger for large trucks
 C: Checked with the rear-view mirror

Correct Answer: B: Larger for large trucks

13. After a minor collision with a parked vehicle, and the owner is absent, you must:
 A: Leave a note
 B: Report to the police or CHP
 C: Both of the above

Correct Answer: C: Both of the above

14. Unless posted otherwise, the speed limit in residential areas is:
 A: 20 mph
 B: 25 mph
 C: 30 mph

Correct Answer B: 25 mph

15. Legally blocking an intersection is allowed:
 A: On a green light
 B: During rush hour
 C: Under no circumstances

Correct Answer: C: Under no circumstances

16. When parking uphill on a curbless two-way street, your front wheels should be turned:
 A: Left toward the street
 B: Right away from the street

C: Parallel with the pavement

Correct Answer: B: Right away from the street

17. With a Class C driver's license, you may drive a three-axle vehicle if the gross vehicle weight is less than:
   A: 6,000 pounds
   B: Any weight for a three-axle vehicle
   C: A vehicle pulling two trailers

Correct Answer: A: 6,000 pounds

18. When turning left from a multi-lane one-way street to another one-way street, start your turn from:
   A: Any lane, if safe
   B: The lane closest to the left curve
   C: The center lane

Correct Answer: B: The lane closest to the left curve

19. If involved in a traffic collision, you must submit a written report (SR1) to the DMV if there is property damage exceeding:
   A: Only if there are injuries
   B: Exceeding $1,000 or if there are injuries
   C: Only if you are at fault

Correct Answer: B: Exceeding $1,000 or if there are injuries

20. Roadways are most slippery:
   A: During a heavy downpour
   B: After prolonged rain
   C: The first rain after a dry spell

Correct Answer: C: The first rain after a dry spell

21. Where may you not park your vehicle?
   A: Side of the freeway in an emergency
   B: Next to a red-painted curve

C: Within 100 feet of an elementary school

Correct Answer: B: Next to a red-painted curve

22. When must you notify the DMV within five days?
    A: Sell or transfer your vehicle
    B: Fail a smog test for your vehicle
    C: Get a new prescription for lenses or contacts

Correct Answer: A: Sell or transfer your vehicle

23. Two sets of solid double yellow lines that are two or more feet apart:
    A: May be crossed to enter or exit a private driveway
    B: May not be crossed for any reason
    C: Should be treated as a separate traffic lane

Correct Answer: B: May not be crossed for any reason

24. Making a right turn at an upcoming intersection, you should slow down and:
    A: Move toward the left side of your lane
    B: Avoid driving in the bicycle lane
    C: Signal for 100 feet before turning

Correct Answer: C: Signal for 100 feet before turning

25. Driving on a freeway posted for 65 mph, with traffic at 70 mph, you may legally drive:
    A: 70 mph or faster to keep up with traffic
    B: Between 65 mph and 70 mph
    C: No faster than 65 mph

Correct Answer: C: No faster than 65 mph

26. It is not permitted to park your car.
    A: In an unmarked crosswalk
    B: Within three feet of a private driveway
    C: In a bicycle lane

Correct Answer: A: In an unmarked crosswalk

27. The safest precaution for using cellular phones and driving is.
    A: Use hands-free devices to keep both hands on the steering wheel
    B: Keep your phone within easy reach to avoid looking away
    C: Review the number before answering a call

Correct Answer: A: Use hands-free devices to keep both hands on the steering wheel

28. If you have a green light but the intersection is blocked, you should:
    A: Stay out of the intersection until traffic clears
    B: Enter the intersection and wait until traffic clears
    C: Merge into another lane and try to go around the traffic

Correct Answer: A: Stay out of the intersection until traffic clears

29. Getting ready to make a right turn, you should:
    A: Signal and turn immediately
    B: Stop before entering the right lane and let other traffic go first
    C: Slow down or stop if necessary and then make the turn

Correct Answer: C: Slow down or stop if necessary and then make the turn

30. School crossing guards have instructions that you must follow:
    A: At all times
    B: Only during school hours
    C: Unless you do not see any children present

Correct Answer: A: At all times

31. On a windy day with reduced visibility due to a dust storm, you should drive slower and turn on your:
    A: Interior lights
    B: Parking lights
    C: Headlights

Correct Answer: C: Headlights

32. When planning to pass another vehicle, you should:
    A: Not assume the other driver will make space for you to return
    B: Assume the other driver will let you pass if you use your turn signal
    C: Assume the other driver will maintain a constant speed

  Correct Answer: A: Not assume the other driver will make space for you to return

33. When an emergency vehicle's siren sounds while you are at a crosswalk, you ought to.
    A: Move to the right and stop at the intersection
    B: Continue through the intersection, then move to the right and stop
    C: Continue through the intersection, then move to the left and stop

  Correct Answer: B: Continue through the intersection, then move to the right and stop

34. Driving faster than other vehicles on a single-lane road and continually passing them will:
    A: Get you to your destination much faster and safer
    B: Increase your chances of an accident
    C: Help prevent traffic congestion

  Correct Answer: B: Increase your chances of an accident

35. Vehicles that must always stop before crossing railroad tracks include:
    A: Tank trucks marked with hazardous materials placards
    B: Motorhomes or pickup trucks towing a boat trailer
     C: Any vehicle with three or more axles or weighing more than four thousand pounds

  Correct Answer: A: Tank trucks marked with hazardous materials placards

36. On a one-way street, you may turn left onto another one-way street only if:
    A: Sign permits the turn
    B: Traffic on the street moves to the right
    C: Traffic on the street moves to the left

Correct Answer: C: Traffic on the street moves to the left

37. When a large truck is turning right onto a street with two lanes in each direction, the truck:
    A: May complete its turn in either of the two lanes
    B: May have to swing wide to complete the right turn
    C: Must stay in the right lane at all times while turning

Correct Answer: B: May have to swing wide to complete the right turn

38. In order to pass another car, you may cross a double yellow line if the yellow line adjacent to:
    A: The other side of the road is a solid line
    B: Your side of the road is a broken line
    C: The other side of the road is a broken line

Correct Answer: B: Your side of the road is a broken line

39. When it comes to railroad crossings, crosswalks, and intersections, you should always:
    A: Stop, listen, and proceed cautiously
    B: Look to the sides of your vehicle to see what is coming
    C: Slowly pass vehicles that seem to be stopped for no reason

Correct Answer: B: Look to the sides of your vehicle to see what is coming

40. Driving defensively involves:
    A: Always putting one car length between you and the car ahead
    B: Looking only at the car in front of you while driving
    C: Keeping your eyes moving to look for possible hazards

Correct Answer: C: Keeping your eyes moving to look for possible hazards

41. When driving on the freeway behind a large truck, you should drive:
    A: Closely behind the truck in bad weather because the driver can see farther ahead
    B: Farther behind the truck than you would for a passenger vehicle
    C: No more than one car length behind the truck so the driver can see you

Correct Answer: B: Farther behind the truck than you would for a passenger vehicle

42. All of the following practices are dangerous while driving. Which is also illegal?
    A: Listening to music through headphones that cover both ears
    B: Adjusting your outside mirrors
    C: Transporting an unrestrained animal inside the vehicle

Correct Answer: A: Listening to music through headphones that cover both ears

43. Never cross railroad tracks without stopping first when.
    A: You don't have room on the other side to completely cross the tracks
    B: The railroad crossing is located in a city or town that has frequent train traffic
    C: You transport two or more young children in a passenger vehicle

Correct Answer: A: You don't have room on the other side to completely cross the tracks

44. When you tailgate other drivers by driving close to their rear bumper:
    A: You can frustrate the other drivers and make them angry
    B: Your actions cannot result in a traffic citation
    C: You help reduce traffic congestion

Correct Answer: A: You can frustrate the other drivers and make them angry

45. Must you always travel at a slower speed than other vehicles?
    A: No, you can block traffic when you drive too slowly
    B: Yes, it is a good defensive driving technique
    C: Yes, it is always safer than driving faster than other traffic

Correct Answer: A: No, you can block traffic when you drive too slowly

46. When you see a single person at a road construction site ahead, you should obey his or her instructions:
    A: Only if you see orange cones on the road ahead
    B: Unless they conflict with existing signs, signals, or laws
    C: At all times

Correct Answer: C: At all times

47. How long is it legal to drive in a bike lane?
    A: If there are no cyclists in the bike lane during rush hour.
    B: When you are 200 feet or less from a cross street where you want to turn right.
    C: When you want to pass a driver ahead of you who is turning right

Correct Answer: B: When you are 200 feet or less from a cross street where you want to turn right.

48. If you see a flashing yellow traffic signal at an upcoming intersection, the flashing yellow light means:
    A: Stop before entering the intersection as long as you can do so safely
    B: Stop, yield to all cross traffic before crossing the intersection
    C: Slow down and cross the intersection carefully

Correct Answer: C: Slow down and cross the intersection carefully

49. A pedestrian is crossing your lane in front of you, but there is no crosswalk. How ought one to proceed?
    A: Make eye contact and then pass him or her
    B: Slow down as you pass him or her
    C: Stop and let him or her finish crossing the street

Correct Answer: C: Stop and let him or her finish crossing the street

Practice Tests 3

1. What is a safety zone?
    A: An empty lane next to the freeway dividers
    B: A space set aside for pedestrians
    C: The meridian strip on a divided highway

Correct Answer: B: A space set aside for pedestrians

2. If you get sleepy while driving, you should:

A: Drive to a safe place, stop, and rest
B: Play the audio loudly and roll down the windows
C: Drink coffee to make you more alert

Correct Answer: A: Drive to a safe place, stop, and rest

3. The motorist in front of you comes to a stop at a crosswalk. What should you do?
A: Drive to the right edge of the road and stop
B: Stop, then proceed when safe
C: Change lanes, look carefully, and pass

Correct Answer: B: Stop, then proceed when safe

4. You are stopped at an intersection, and the traffic light just turned green. Can you go immediately?
A: Yes, other traffic or pedestrians must yield to you
B: Yes, you now have the right of way
C: Yes, but yield to any vehicle or person still in the intersection

Correct Answer: C: Yes, but yield to any vehicle or person still in the intersection

5. Signal for a turn during the last ___ feet before the turn.
A: 100
B: 50
C: 75

Correct Answer: A: 100

6. When should a three-year-old weighing 45 pounds be placed in a safety seat?
A: Under all circumstances
B: Only when driving on the freeway
C: Only if the child is in the front seat

Correct Answer: A: Under all circumstances

7. This sign means:

A: The driver on the right goes first

B: All other drivers go first

C: Make a complete stop before turning

Correct Answer: B: All other drivers go first

8. A solid yellow line adjacent to a broken yellow line indicates that vehicles:

A: In both directions may pass

B: Next to the broken line may pass

C: Next to the solid line may pass

Correct Answer: B: Next to the broken line may pass

9. A curb painted red means:

A: Parking is for emergency vehicles only

B: Parking is for disabled persons only

C: Stopping or parking is not allowed except for buses

Correct Answer: C: Stopping or parking is not allowed except for buses

10. This sign means:

A: Right lane ends ahead

B: No right turn

C: Side road to the right

Correct Answer: B: No right turn

11. Which of the following is true about double parking?

A: It is allowed if you are making a delivery.

B: It is illegal under all circumstances.
C: It is illegal unless you wait in the vehicle.

Correct Answer: B: It is illegal under all circumstances.

12. It is illegal for a person 21 years of age or older to drive with a blood alcohol concentration that is ___ or more.
   A: One-tenth of one percent.
   B: Eight hundredths of one percent.
   C: Five hundredths of one percent.

Correct Answer: B: Eight hundredths of one percent

13. You should use a turnout lane when:
   A: You want to pass another driver.
   B: You want to make a U-turn.
   C: Faster drivers want to pass you.

 Correct Answer: C: Faster drivers want to pass you

14. This sign means:
   A: Crossroad intersects the main road.
   B: Divided highway ahead.
   C: Fewer lanes ahead.

Correct Answer: B: Divided highway ahead

15. You are driving at night and using high beams. Dim your lights when you get closer than ___ feet from the car ahead.
   A: 300.
   B: 200.
   C: 400.

Correct Answer: A: 300

16. You have been involved in a minor traffic collision with a parked vehicle and can't find the owner. You must:
   A: Leave a note on the vehicle.

B: Report the accident without delay to the city police or, in unincorporated areas, to the CHP.

C: Both of the above.

correct Answer: C: Both of the above.

17. Do you need to signal when you pull away from the curb?

A: No, you only need to signal when you approach the curve.

B: Yes, you need to signal when you pull away from the curb.

C: if there are other vehicles around you.

Correct Answer: Option B: Yes, you need to always signal when you pull away from the curb.

18. Wh Men driving, you must turn on your headlights:

A: Whenever you turn on your wipers due to adverse weather conditions.

B: 30 minutes after sunset and 30 minutes before sunrise.

C: Both of the above.

Correct Answer: Option C: Both of the above.

19. Which of these statements is true about safety zones?

A: The road is probably being repaired by slow-moving vehicles.

B: If a streetcar is stopped at the safety zone controlled by a traffic signal, you can pass at 25 miles per hour.

C: It is a space set aside for pedestrians and marked by raised buttons or road markings.

Correct Answer: C: It is a space set aside for pedestrians and marked by raised buttons or road markings.

20. There is a railroad crossing ahead, and you can't see if any trains are coming until you are almost ready to cross the tracks. How fast should you be driving?

A: 10 miles per hour.

B: 15 miles per hour.

C: 25 miles per hour.

Correct Answer: B: 15 miles per hour.

21. The intersection has a stop sign. Where should you first stop?
   A: At the crosswalk or limit line.
   B: After the crosswalk.
   C: Out far enough to see the cross traffic.

Correct Answer: A: At the crosswalk or limit line.

22. What is the benefit of a space cushion around your vehicle?
   A: If another driver makes a mistake, you have time to react.
   B: There is none; other drivers just crowd in front of you.
   C: You don't have to worry about the driver next to you.

Correct Answer: A: If another driver makes a mistake, you have time to react.

23. If you have a conditional driver's license, there are:
   A: A special time limit to renew your license.
   B: Special restrictions you must follow when driving.
   C: Age limits imposed on your driver's license.

Correct Answer: B: Special restrictions you must follow when driving.

24. This warning sign means:

   A: Winding road ahead begins with a curve to the left.
   B: Passing allowed from left and right.
   C: Winding road ahead begins with a curve to the right.

Correct Answer: C: Winding road ahead begins with a curve to the right.

25. When is it required to signal before changing lanes?
   A: At all times.
   B: Only when there are other vehicles nearby.
   C: Only when changing lanes on a freeway.

Correct Answer: A: At all times.

26. This sign means:

    A: U-turn area ahead.
    B: No U-turn.
    C: No passing.

Correct Answer: B: No U-turn.

27. You can drive in the carpool lane if you:
    A: Are driving an empty 15-passenger van.
    B: Want to pass the vehicle ahead.
    C: Have the minimum number of passengers shown on the sign.

Correct Answer: C: Have the minimum number of passengers shown on the sign.

28. The speed limit for a school zone where children are present is ___ unless otherwise posted.
    A: 15 miles per hour.
    B: 25 miles per hour.
    C: 20 miles per hour.

Correct Answer: B: 25 miles per hour.

29. Which way do you turn your front wheels to park uphill next to a curve?
    A: Parallel to the curve.
    B: To the left, away from the curve.
    C: To the right, into the curve.

Correct Answer: B: To the left, away from the curve.

30. You can avoid skidding on a slippery surface by:
    A: Shifting to a lower gear after you start down a steep hill.
    B: Following in the tracks of the vehicle in front of you.

C: Slowing down as you approach curves and intersections.

Correct Answer: C: Slowing down as you approach curves and intersections.

31. A driver unexpectedly pulls in front of you. The handbook recommends:
    A: Swerving into the lane next to you.
    B: Driving onto the shoulder of the road.
    C: Taking your foot off the gas pedal.

Correct Answer: C: Taking your foot off the gas pedal.

32. You sold your vehicle. You must notify Dash within five days.
    A: Your insurance company.
    B: DMV.
    C: The automobile club.

Correct Answer: B: DMV.

33. Which of these statements is true about large trucks?
    A: Trucks are not as maneuverable as passenger vehicles.
    B: They do not need more space to stop and start.
    C: They do not need more space for turns.

Correct Answer: A: Trucks are not as maneuverable as passenger vehicles.

34. You are driving on a highway, your tire suddenly goes flat, and you need to pull over and get help. Where should you pull over?
    A: In the right-hand lane.
    B: Wherever your car will be visible for 200 feet from the front.
    C: Off the pavement.

Correct Answer: C: Off the pavement.

35. You are repeatedly convicted of traffic violations. What can happen?
    A: DMV may suspend your driving privilege.
    B: MV may revoke your insurance.
    C: DMV will suspend the registration of your vehicle.

Correct Answer: A: DMV may suspend your driving privilege.

36. To turn left from a multi-lane one-way street onto a one-way street, you should start your turn from:
    A: Any lane as long as it is safe.
    B: The lane closest to the left curve.
    C: The lane in the center of the road.

Correct Answer: B: The lane closest to the left curve.

37. You should check traffic behind you:
    A: So you will know if you are being followed by a tailgater.
    B: Only on the freeway or highway.
    C: Only when you are slowing down.

Correct Answer: A: So you will know if you are being followed by a tailgater.

38. This sign means:

    A: The driver on the right goes first.
    B: All other drivers go first.
    C: Make a complete stop before turning.

Correct Answer: B: All other drivers go first.

39. A railroad crossing is up ahead. A mechanical signal alerts you to the impending train. You have to:
    A: Stop, then proceed when safe.
    B: Slow down before crossing.
    C: Stop only if you see a train coming.

Correct Answer: A: Stop, then proceed when safe.

40. If you are involved in a traffic collision, you are required to complete and submit a written report (SR1) to the DMV:

A: Only if you or the other driver is injured.

B: If there is property damage in excess of $1,000 or if there are any injuries.

C: Only if you are at fault.

Correct Answer: B: If there is property damage in excess of $1,000 or if there are any injuries.

41. You want to back out of an angle parking space. You should always back slowly and:

A: Look at your rearview mirror.

B: Have someone outside of the vehicle direct you.

C: Look over your right shoulder.

Correct Answer: C: Look over your right shoulder.

42. You are driving 55 miles per hour on a two-lane road and want to pass the car ahead of you. To pass safely, you need a dash gap in the oncoming traffic.

A: Five seconds.

B: Seven seconds.

C: 10 to 12 seconds.

Correct Answer: C: 10 to 12 seconds.

43. Parking is never permitted.

A: 20 feet from a railroad track.

B: On a hill.

C: In a cross-hatched pattern space next to a disabled parking space.

Correct Answer: C: In a cross-hatched pattern space next to a disabled parking space.

44. Yellow lines separate:

A: Traffic lanes on one-way streets.

B: Traffic moving in opposite directions on two-way roads.

C: A lane barrier between regular and carpool lanes.

Correct Answer: B: Traffic moving in opposite directions on two-way roads.

45. A person can ride in the back of a pickup truck when:

A: Pickup bed has a seat bolted to the frame.
B: Sides of the pickup bed are at least 24 inches high.
C: Back of the pickup is equipped with a restraint system.

Correct Answer: C: Back of the pickup is equipped with a restraint system.

46. What should you do when a road sign states that headlights must be on?
   A: Ignore the sign and continue driving if it is a sunny day.
   B: Turn on your high beam headlights.
   C: Turn on your low beam headlights.

Correct Answer: C: Turn on your low beam headlights.

Practice Tests 4

1. It is illegal for a person 21 years of age or older to drive with a blood alcohol concentration that is Dash or more.
   A: 1/10th of 1%
   B: 8 hundredths of 1%
   C: 5 hundredths of 1%

Correct Answer: B: 8 hundredths of 1%

2. Within five days, you have to let DMV know whether you:
   A: Sell or transfer your vehicle.
   B: Paint your vehicle a different color.
   C: Are cited for a traffic violation.

Correct Answer: A: Sell or transfer your vehicle.

3. There is an uncontrolled T intersection that two cars are approaching. The two vehicles are on the route that terminates and the through road. At the crossroads, who has the right-of-way?
   A: The vehicle on the through road.
   B: The vehicle on the right.
   C: The vehicle that arrives first.

Correct Answer: A: The vehicle on the through road.

4. When a traffic signal light isn't working at an intersection, you should:
    A: Come to a complete stop then proceed when it is safe.
    B: Stop before entering and let all other traffic go first.
    C: Slow down or stop if necessary.

Correct Answer: A: Come to a complete stop then proceed when it is safe.

5. This red and white sign means you should:
    A: Stop and check traffic both ways before proceeding.
    B: Give way to oncoming traffic on the road you want to cross or enter.
     C: Keep a steady speed and check traffic both ways.

Correct Answer: B: Give way to oncoming traffic on the road you want to cross or enter.

6. If you have a green light but traffic is blocking the intersection:
    A: Stay out of the intersection until traffic clears.
    B: Merge into another lane and try to go around the traffic.
    C: Enter the intersection and wait until traffic clears.

Correct Answer: A: Stay out of the intersection until traffic clears.

7. When someone under the age of eighteen is present, smoking inside a car is:
    A: Legal if it is your child.
    B: Illegal at all times.
    C: Not restricted by law.

Correct Answer: B: Illegal at all times.

8. When is it legal to use a cell phone without a hands-free device while driving:
    A: When making a call while stopped at a red light.
    B: When making a call for emergency assistance.
    C: Never.

Correct Answer: B: When making a call for emergency assistance.

9. Which statement is true about motorcyclists and motorists:

A: Motorcyclists are not allowed to drive faster than other traffic during congested road conditions.

B: Motorcyclists have the same rights and responsibilities as other motorists.

C: Motorcycles are heavier than other vehicles and are less affected by wind or rain.

Correct Answer: B: Motorcyclists have the same rights and responsibilities as other motorists.

10. You should stop before crossing railroad tracks:

A: Even when the railroad tracks are out of service.

B: Anytime a train may be approaching, whether or not you can see it.

C: If your vehicle has three or more axles.

Correct Answer: B: Anytime a train may be approaching, whether or not you can see it.

11. You are getting ready to make a right turn. You should:

A: Always stop before making a right turn.

B: Signal during the last 100 ft before you turn.

C: Slow down and signal as you start your turn.

Correct Answer: B: Signal during the last 100 ft before you turn.

12. The car in front of you is turning left into a driveway on a two-way street. It is lawful for you to pass the car on the right:

A: If there is enough road between the curve and the vehicle.

B: Even if you must drive in a bicycle lane to do so.

C: Even if you must cross a solid white line painted on the road.

Correct Answer: A: If there is enough road between the curb and the vehicle.

13. The speed limit in any alley is:

A: 20 mph.

B: 15 mph.

C: 25 mph.

Correct Answer: B: 15 mph.

14. To turn left from a multi-lane one-way street onto a one-way street, you should start your turn from:

    A: Any lane as long as it is safe.

    B: The lane closest to the left curve.

    C: The lane in the center of the road.

Correct Answer: B: The lane closest to the left curve.

15. Which of these statements is true about child passengers:

    A: Children one or older and over 20 pounds should ride in the front seat.

    B: Children under age 1 should not ride in the front seat in airbag-equipped vehicles.

    C: The front seat is generally the safest place in the car for children 6 years of age and older.

Correct Answer: B: Children under age 1 should not ride in the front seat in airbag-equipped vehicles.

16. When you change lanes or merge with another lane, you:

    A: Have the right of way.

    B: Should first stop and check for cross traffic.

    C: Need at least a 4-second gap in traffic.

Correct Answer: C: Need at least a 4-second gap in traffic.

17. This white sign means:

    A: Railroad crossing is controlled; continue at your regular speed.

    B: Look, listen, and prepare to stop at the crossing if necessary.

    C: Stop at the railroad tracks and wait for a signal before crossing.

Correct Answer: B: Look, listen, and prepare to stop at the crossing if necessary.

18. If there is a deep puddle in the road ahead, you should:

    A: Maintain the posted speed to make it through the water.

B: Avoid the puddle if possible.

C: Shift into neutral as you drive through the water.

Correct Answer: B: Avoid the puddle if possible.

19. You must make a written report of a traffic accident occurring in California (SR1) to DMV if you:

A: Fail to pay your registration fees within 90 days of receiving your renewal notice.

B: Are involved in a collision, and there is more than $1,000 in damages.

C: Allow a licensed driver from another state to drive your vehicle.

Correct Answer: B: Are involved in a collision, and there is more than $1,000 in damages.

20. You are driving in the far-right lane of a four-lane freeway and notice thick broken white lines on the left side of your lane. You are driving in:

A: The carpool lane and must merge into the next lane.

B: A special lane for slow-moving vehicles.

C: An exit lane.

Correct Answer: C: An exit lane.

21. Which of these statements is true about driving and taking medications?

A: Most cold medications can make a person drowsy.

B: Over-the-counter medications cannot impair driving ability if taken in the recommended dosages.

C: Medications are safe to take at any time if prescribed by a doctor.

Correct Answer: A: Most cold medications can make a person drowsy.

22. Which of the following is true about large trucks?

A: Trucks have fewer blind spots due to the vehicle's height.

B: It is best to pass trucks very slowly and on the right side.

C: Trucks often appear to travel slower because of their large size.

Correct Answer: C: Trucks often appear to travel slower because of their large size.

23. Which of the following traffic signals requires you to stop your car every time?
    A: Solid red lights, flashing red lights, and blacked-out traffic signals.
    B: Solid red lights, red arrows, and flashing yellow lights.
    C: Solid red lights, flashing red lights, and yellow lights.

Correct Answer: A: Solid red lights, flashing red lights, and blacked-out traffic signals.

24. Upon noticing this yellow sign, you ought to:
    A: Always stop at the crosswalk.
    B: Stop at the crosswalk until a crossing guard signals you to go.
    C: Be prepared to stop if children are in the crosswalk.

Correct Answer: C: Be prepared to stop if children are in the crosswalk.

25. When considering whether to cross the street, a blind or visually challenged person listens for traffic noises. When you witness a person waiting to cross at an intersection with a white cane or guide dog, you should:
    A: Stop at the crosswalk and honk your horn.
    B: Drive into the crosswalk so the person can hear your engine.
    C: Pull up to the crosswalk so the person can hear your engine.

Correct Answer: C: Pull up to the crosswalk so the person can hear your engine.

26. You should drive directly ahead with your wheels unless you are:
    A: Waiting to make a left turn at a traffic light.
    B: Parked on a hill or sloping driveway.
    C: Parked on the side of a level roadway and there is no curve.

Correct Answer: B: Parked on a hill or sloping driveway.

27. In a moving car, you have to wear your safety belt.:
    A: Unless the vehicle was manufactured before 1975.
    B: Unless you are riding in the back of a pickup camper.
    C: And failure to do so will result in a traffic ticket.

Correct Answer: C: And failure to do so will result in a traffic ticket.

28. When driving in fog, snow, or rain, you should use your:
    A: Low beam headlights.
    B: High beam headlights.
    C: Running lights.

Correct Answer: A: Low beam headlights.

29. To be sure a lane is clear before you change lanes, you should:
    A: Look in your outside mirrors only.
    B: Glance over your shoulder into the lane you want to enter.
    C: Always turn your head and look over your right shoulder.

Correct Answer: B: Glance over your shoulder into the lane you want to enter.

30. You should adjust your rearview and side mirrors:
    A: Before you get into the car.
    B: Before you start driving.
    C: After you start driving.

Correct Answer: B: Before you start driving.

31. Cargo extending more than 4 ft from your rear bumper:
    A: Is illegal under all circumstances.
    B: Has to be indicated with lights or a red flag.
    C: Does not legally have to be marked but it is a good idea.

Correct Answer: B: Has to be indicated with lights or a red flag.

32. The speed limit for a school zone where children are present is:
    A: 15 mph.
    B: 25 mph.
    C: 20 mph.

Correct Answer: B: 25 mph.

33. Instructions from school crossing guards must be obeyed:
    A: At all times.

B: During school hours only.

C: Only when children are present in front of a school.

Correct Answer: A: At all times.

34. You are crossing an intersection and an emergency vehicle is approaching with a siren and flashing lights. You should:

A: Stop immediately in the intersection until it passes.

B: Pull to the right in the intersection and stop.

C: Continue through the intersection, pull to the right, and stop.

Correct Answer: C: Continue through the intersection, pull to the right, and stop.

35. You are being signaled to pull over to the side of the road by a peace officer. You choose to depart the scene and disobey the officer's warning. You have committed a misdemeanor and may face the following penalties:

A: Fined up to $1,000.

B: Jailed in the county jail for not more than one year.

C: Given a warning and a citation.

Correct Answer: B: Jailed in the county jail for not more than one year.

36. All of the following are dangerous while driving, which is also illegal:

A: Wearing a headset that covers both ears.

B: Having one or more interior lights on.

C: Using cruise control on residential streets.

Correct Answer: A: Wearing a headset that covers both ears.

37. This sign on a center lane means you may use this lane for:

A: Turning left or right only.

B: Passing slow-moving vehicles only.

C: Turning left only.

Correct Answer: C: Turning left only.

38. During a traffic stop, what documents should you be prepared to provide to law enforcement:

A: Only your driver's license.

B: Your driver's license, vehicle registration, and proof of insurance.

C: None, as law enforcement has access to your information.

Correct Answer: B: Your driver's license, vehicle registration, and proof of insurance.

39. You are driving on a two-lane road and want to pass the vehicle in front of you. To pass safely, you need:

A: A gap large enough for your vehicle to completely pass the other vehicle without exceeding the speed limit.

B: A gap that is only slightly larger than the other vehicle.

C: A gap that is two car lengths long.

Correct Answer: A: A gap large enough for your vehicle to completely pass the other vehicle without exceeding the speed limit.

40. If you are convicted of driving under the influence in California, you may be required to:

A: Pay a fine, attend DUI school, and have your license suspended or revoked.

B: Only pay a fine.

C: Attend traffic school and have your license reinstated immediately.

Correct Answer: A: Pay a fine, attend DUI school, and have your license suspended or revoked.

41. When you see a solid white line between lanes of traffic, you should:

A: Stay within your lane.

B: Change lanes only when it's safe to do so.

C: Merge into another lane immediately.

Correct Answer: A: Stay within your lane.

42. When making a left turn at an intersection and there is a green arrow signal:

A: You should turn without checking for traffic.

B: You must yield to oncoming traffic.

C: You have the right of way and can turn safely.

Correct Answer: C: You have the right of way and can turn safely.

43. You are approaching an intersection with a green traffic light, pedestrians are crossing against the red signal. You should:
     A: Stop and wait for the pedestrians to cross.
     B: Sound your horn to alert the pedestrians.
     C: Drive around the pedestrians to proceed through the intersection.

Correct Answer: A: Stop and wait for the pedestrians to cross

44. When approaching a stopped emergency vehicle with its lights flashing on a highway with two lanes in the same direction, you must:
     A: Slow down and proceed with caution.
     B: Maintain your speed and pass the emergency vehicle quickly.
     C: Change lanes to the left if safe or slow down and proceed with caution.

 Correct Answer: C: Change lanes to the left if safe or slow down and proceed with caution.

45. You're traveling down a divided highway with many lanes. If you must do a U-turn, you should:
     A: Make the U-turn from the far left lane.
     B: Make the U-turn from the center lane.
     C: Make the U-turn from the right lane.

Correct Answer: A: Make the U-turn from the far left lane.

46. Which of the following is a legal U-turn:
     A: On a divided highway where there is a paved opening for a turn.
     B: 150-foot distance from a slope or bend.
     C: In a residential area where there are no vehicles approaching within 500 ft.

Correct Answer: : On a divided highway where there is a paved opening for a turn.

47. If you are involved in a collision and no one is injured, you should:
     A: Exchange information with the other party and leave the scene.
     B: Move your vehicle off the road if possible and call for assistance.

C: Leave your vehicle in the traffic lane until the police arrive.

Correct Answer: B: Move your vehicle off the road if possible and call for assistance.

48. When a school bus is stopped with its red lights flashing, you must stop:
    A: If you are on a divided highway.
    B: Unless you are on the other side of a divided or multi-lane highway.
    C: Only if children are crossing the road.

Correct Answer: B: Unless you are on the other side of a divided or multi-lane highway.

Practice Tests 5

1. What does a single solid yellow line on a road indicate?
    A: The center of a road with two-way traffic.
    B: A lane barrier between regular and preferential use lanes.
    C: Separation between two lanes going in the same direction.

Correct Answer: A: The center of a road with two-way traffic.

2. What does a solid yellow line on your side of the road mean?
    A: Passing is allowed.
    B: Passing is not allowed.
    C: Passing is allowed only in certain circumstances.

Correct Answer: B: Passing is not allowed.

3. What does a broken yellow line indicate?
    A: Lane barrier between regular and preferential use lanes.
    B: The center of a road with two-way traffic.
    C: You may pass if the broken line is next to your driving lane.

Correct Answer: C: You may pass if the broken line is next to your driving lane.

4. What does a single solid white line indicate?
   A: The center of a road with two-way traffic.
   B: Separation between two lanes going in the same direction.
   C: A lane barrier between regular and preferential use lanes.

Correct Answer: B: Separation between two lanes going in the same direction.

5. What does a broken white line on the road mean?
   A: Passing is allowed.
   B: Passing is not allowed.
   C: Passing is allowed only in certain circumstances.

Correct Answer: A: Passing is allowed.

6. What do double solid white lines indicate?
   A: A lane barrier between regular and preferential use lanes.
   B: Separation between two lanes going in the same direction.
   C: A lane for emergency vehicles only.

Correct Answer: A: A lane barrier between regular and preferential use lanes.

7. What does a double solid yellow line on the road mean?
   A: Passing is allowed on both sides of the road.
   B: Passing is allowed only on one side of the road.
   C: Passing is not allowed on either side of the road.

Correct Answer: C: Passing is not allowed on either side of the road.

8. What does a white diamond painted on the road mean?
   A: High Occupancy Vehicle (HOV) lane.
   B: Pedestrian crossing.
   C: Bike lane.

Correct Answer: A: High Occupancy Vehicle (HOV) lane.

9. On a multi-lane road with lanes separated by single solid white lines, passing is:
   A: Allowed.

B: Not allowed.

C: Allowed only in certain circumstances.

Correct Answer: B: Not allowed.

10. Which of these is an illegal U-turn?

A: On a divided highway where there is a paved opening for a turn.

B: 150 feet away from a hill or curve.

C: Over two sets of double yellow lines in the roadway.

Correct Answer: C: Over two sets of double yellow lines in the roadway.

11. If there are two solid yellow lines dividing opposite lanes of traffic, you may:

A: Cross over the lines to make a left turn from or into a side street.

 B: Cross over the lines to pass another vehicle as long as a no passing sign is not posted.

C: Not cross over these lines for any reason.

Correct Answer: C: Not cross over these lines for any reason.

Solid yellow lines indicate that it is not safe to pass, and crossing over the lines is generally not allowed.

12. You can cross double yellow lines to pass another vehicle if the:

A: Vehicle in front of you moves to the right to let you pass.

B: Yellow line next to your side of the road is broken.

C: Yellow line next to the other side of the road is broken.

Correct Answer: B: Yellow line next to your side of the road is broken.

Crossing double yellow lines to pass is allowed only when the line next to your side of the road is broken, indicating that passing is permitted.

13. You are driving at 55 miles per hour on a two-lane highway and want to pass the vehicle ahead of you. To pass safely, you need to:

A: Wait until solid double yellow lines separate the lanes.

B: Increase your speed to at least 60 miles per hour.

C: Have a large enough gap in the oncoming traffic.

Correct Answer: C: Have a large enough gap in the oncoming traffic.

Passing on a two-lane road should be done when there is a clear view ahead and a sufficient gap in oncoming traffic.

14. You are driving on a five-lane freeway in the lane closest to the center divider. To exit the freeway on the right, you should:
    A: Carefully cross all the lanes at one time.
    B: Change lanes one at a time until you are in the proper lane.
    C: Slow down before beginning each lane change.

Correct Answer: B: Change lanes one at a time until you are in the proper lane.

When exiting the freeway, changing lanes one at a time until reaching the proper exit lane is the safe and recommended approach.

15. You must turn on your headlights:
    A: Only when it is completely dark outside.
    B: When it is too dark to see from one thousand feet away.
    C: When it is too dark to see from 500 feet away.

Correct Answer: B: When it is too dark to see from one thousand feet away.

Using headlights when visibility is reduced can improve safety and ensure compliance with legal requirements.

16. When can you drive using only parking lights?
    A: 30 minutes after sunset or 30 minutes before sunrise.
    B: On foggy days.
    C: Not under any circumstances.

Correct Answer: C: Not under any circumstances.

Driving with only parking lights can impair visibility and is generally not allowed for normal driving.

17. You're utilizing your high beams while driving at night on a poorly lit roadway. Dimming your lights is advised when you are 500 feet or less from:
   A: A vehicle approaching you from behind.
   B: An oncoming vehicle.
   C: A sharp curve or hill.

Correct Answer: B: An oncoming vehicle.

Dimming your high beams when approaching an oncoming vehicle helps prevent blinding the other driver.

18. When you need to use your windshield wipers due to fog, rain, or snow, you must:
   A: Turn on your low beam headlights.
   B: Turn on your high beam headlights.
   C: Turn on your emergency flashers.

Correct Answer: A: Turn on your low beam headlights.

Using low beam headlights in adverse weather conditions improves visibility and complies with legal requirements.

19. What is the best driving advise in the event of severe fog or dust?
   A: Try not to drive until the conditions improve.
   B: Do not drive too slowly because other drivers may hit you.
   C: Alternate your low and high beams to improve your vision.

Correct Answer: A: Try not to drive until the conditions improve.

Driving in heavy fog or dust can be hazardous, and waiting for improved conditions is a safe choice.

20. When should you turn on your headlights on mountain roads and tunnels?
   A: Only on cloudy days.
   B: Only at night.
   C: Always, regardless of weather conditions.

Correct Answer: C: Always, regardless of weather conditions.

Headlights improve visibility, especially in poorly lit areas such as tunnels or mountain roads.

21. You should tap your brake pedal three or four times when:
    A: You want to warn other drivers about a hazard ahead.
    B: You need to stop quickly.
    C: You want to make a right turn.

Correct Answer: A: You want to warn other drivers about a hazard ahead.

Brake tapping or brake checking can be used as a warning signal to other drivers about slowing down or stopping.

22. You should turn off your high beam headlights and turn on your low beam headlights when you are:
    A: Within 500 feet of an oncoming vehicle.
    B: Within 300 feet of a vehicle you're following.
    C: Both of the above.

Correct Answer: C: all of the above.

Dimming high beams is necessary both when approaching an oncoming vehicle and when following another vehicle closely.

23. When is it illegal to drive using only parking lights?
    A: At night.
    B: In residential areas.
    C: Always.

Correct Answer: C: Always.

Driving with only parking lights is not sufficient for normal driving and is generally illegal.

24. When driving, you must turn on your headlights:
    A: Whenever you turn on your wipers due to adverse weather conditions.
    B: 30 minutes after sunset and 30 minutes before sunrise.
    C: Both of the above.

Correct Answer: C: all of the above.

Turning on headlights with wipers and during specific times ensures visibility and compliance with regulations.

25. You should turn on your emergency flashers when:
   A: It is raining heavily.
   B: You are driving on a narrow mountain road.
   C: You need to warn other drivers about a collision or hazard ahead.

Correct Answer: C: You need to warn other drivers about a collision or hazard ahead.

Emergency flashers are used to warn other drivers about a hazard or collision ahead.

26. What should you do when you need to stop your vehicle because of vehicle trouble?
   A: Turn on your high beam headlights.
   B: Turn on your emergency flashers.
   C: Use your horn to alert other drivers.

Correct Answer: B: Turn on your emergency flashers.

Turning on your emergency flashers makes your vehicle more visible and helps prevent collisions.

27. Can you use your turn signals instead of emergency flashers if your vehicle doesn't have emergency flashers?
   A: Yes, you can use your turn signals.
   B: No, you should not use your turn signals.
   C: Depending on the circumstances.

Correct Answer: A: Yes, you can use your turn signals.

If your vehicle lacks emergency flashers, using turn signals can serve as a warning to other drivers.

28. What should you do when a road sign states that headlights must be on?

A: Ignore the sign and continue driving if it is a sunny day.
B: Turn on your high beam headlights.
C: Turn on your low beam headlights.

Correct Answer: C: Turn on your low beam headlights.

When a road sign mandates headlights, use your low beams to ensure visibility without blinding others.

29. If it is hard to see one thousand feet ahead of you, what should you do?
    A: Pull over and wait until you can see better.
    B: Turn on your headlights.
    C: Proceed like normal.

Correct Answer: B: Turn on your headlights.

When visibility is reduced, turning on headlights increases your visibility to other drivers and enhances safety.

30. When should you signal before turning?
    A: 50 feet before turning.
    B: 100 feet before turning.
    C: 200 feet before turning.

Correct Answer: B: 100 feet before turning.

According to the United States Department of Transportation, signaling at least 100 feet before turning allows other drivers enough time to react.

31. You should use your turn signals:
    A: When changing lanes or merging into traffic.
    B: When turning left or right.
    C: all of the above.

Correct Answer: C: all of the above.

Turn signals are used when changing lanes, merging into traffic, and when making left or right turns to inform other drivers of your intended actions.

32. What is the proper way to signal when changing lanes?
    A: Signal and immediately change lanes.
    B: Look over your shoulder, then signal, then change lanes.
    C: Change lanes and then signal.

Correct Answer: B: Look over your shoulder, then signal, then change lanes.

Before changing lanes, it's essential to check your blind spot by looking over your shoulder, then signal, and finally, make the lane change when safe.

33. You should turn on your hazard lights when:
    A: Driving in heavy rain or fog.
    B: Your car has broken down on the side of the road.
    C: You are double-parked.

Correct Answer: B: Your car has broken down on the side of the road.

Hazard lights should be used when your vehicle has broken down on the side of the road or in emergency situations.

34. When should you turn off your turn signal?
    A: As soon as you have completed the turn or lane change.
    B: As soon as you begin the turn or lane change.
    C: Before you begin the turn or lane change.

Correct Answer: A: As soon as you have completed the turn or lane change.

Turn off your turn signal promptly after completing the turn or lane change to avoid confusion for other drivers.

35. What happens if you do not signal when required?
    A: You may get a ticket.
    B: You may cause an accident.
    C: All of the above.

Correct Answer: C: All of the above.

Not signaling when required can lead to a ticket and may contribute to accidents.

36. How should bicyclists signal a turn?
   A: Using their vehicle's signal lights.
   B: Using hand and arm positions.
   C: Using their horn.

Correct Answer: B: Using hand and arm positions.

Bicyclists can signal a turn by using hand and arm positions as outlined in traffic regulations.

37. Do you need to signal when you pull away from the curb?
   A: No, you only need to signal when you approach the curb.
   B: Yes, you need to signal when you pull away from the curb.
   C: Only if there are other vehicles around you.

Correct Answer: B: Yes, you need to signal when you pull away from the curb.

Signaling when pulling away from the curb informs other drivers of your intention to merge back into traffic.

38. How long before changing lanes on a freeway should you signal?
   A: Two seconds.
   B: Four seconds.
   C: 5 Seconds.

Correct Answer: C: 5 Seconds.

Signaling at least five seconds before changing lanes on a freeway allows other drivers adequate time to adjust their driving.

39. When is it required to signal before changing lanes?
   A: At all time.
   B: Only when there are other vehicles nearby.
   C: Only when changing lanes on a freeway.

Correct Answer: A: At all times.

Drivers should always signal before changing lanes to communicate intentions and promote safety on the road.

40. What does the below hand signal indicate?
   A: Left turn.
   B: Right turn.
   C: Stop.

Correct Answer: A: Left turn.

41. The left arm and hand extended straight out to the side indicate a left turn. This hand signal is crucial when your vehicle's turn signals are not functional or to communicate intentions to cyclists and pedestrians.

42. What does the below hand signal indicate?
   A: Left turn.
   B: Right turn.
   C: Stop.

Correct Answer: B: Right turn.

43. The hand signal for indicating a right turn is to extend the left arm and hand upward with the palm facing forward. This signal is useful when turn signals are not working, ensuring clear communication with cyclists and pedestrians.

44. What does the below hand signal indicate?
   A: Left turn.
   B: Right turn.
   C: Stop.

Correct Answer: C: Stop.

45. The hand signal for indicating a stop is to extend the left arm and hand downward with the palm facing behind you. This signal is essential when your vehicle's brake lights are not functioning correctly or to communicate stopping intentions to others.

46. You may use your horn on narrow mountain roads:

A: To alert oncoming traffic where you cannot see at least 200 feet ahead.

B: To let pedestrians know you're there.

C: To signal to other drivers that you are in a hurry.

Correct Answer: A: To alert oncoming traffic where you cannot see at least 200 feet ahead.

47. Is it legal to use your horn in residential areas?

A: Yes, as long as you use it during the day.

B: No, it is not legal to use the horn in residential areas unless it is an emergency.

C: It is only legal if you live in the residential area.

Correct Answer: B: No, it is not legal to use the horn in residential areas unless it is an emergency.

48. Using the horn in residential areas is generally not legal unless it is an emergency. Horn use can be disruptive to the peace and quiet of the neighborhood.

49. . What should you do if another driver honks at you?

A: Ignore it and continue driving.

B: Honk back.

C: Make an obscene gesture.

Correct Answer: A: Ignore it and continue driving.

59.. Before making a left or right turn, you should signal for at least:

A: 50 feet.
B: 100 feet.
C: 400 feet.

Correct Answer: B: 100 feet.

Chapter 2: Rules of the Road

Understanding Traffic Signs and Signals

1.Stop Sign

Red octagon with bold white "**STOP**" letters.
Function: Must come to a full stop at intersections to manage traffic flow.

2. Speed Limit Sign

White circle, black numbers indicating maximum speed.
   Function: Informs drivers of permissible speed, posted along roadways to regulate speed.

3. Yield Sign

White triangle with a red border and letters pointing downward.

Function: Requires yielding right of way, used at expressway entrances or merging lanes.

4. No U-Turn Sign

Circular sign, red slash over U-turn symbol.
Function: Prohibits U-turns at specified locations, often where unsafe or disruptive.

5. Railroad Crossing Sign

Yellow round sign with black "X" and two tracks.
Function: Warns of the upcoming railroad crossing, often with flashing lights and barriers.

6. No Parking Sign

White circle, with cross letter P.
Function: Indicates areas where parking is prohibited, near hydrants or busy streets.

7. Do Not Enter Sign

Red circle, white horizontal line, and the clear message **"DO NOT ENTER."**
Function: Restricts entry into specific zones or roads, commonly seen on one-ways or freeway ramps.

8. Pedestrian Crossing Sign

White triangular-shaped sign, black pedestrian symbol.

Function: Warns of upcoming pedestrian crossings, common near schools or crosswalks.

9. Turn Right Only Sign

Square sign, black arrow on yellow, signing "**TURN RIGHT ONLY**."

Function: Specifies right turn at upcoming intersection, often used to regulate traffic.

10. School Zone Sign

Yellow pentagon, black symbol of children.

Function: Alerts to school zone, indicates reduced speed limits when children are present.

11. Warning Sign - Curve Ahead

Yellow diamond, black arrow curving right.

Function: Alerts to the upcoming curved road, and indicates the direction of the curve.

12. No Left Turn Sign

Circle sign, Black arrow on white, signing **"NO LEFT TURN."**
Function: Prohibits left turns at designated locations, often at intersections.

13. Bicycle Lane Sign

Square sign, white bicycle on green.
Function: Designates lanes for bicycle use, found in areas with dedicated bike lanes.

14. Roundabout Sign

Circular sign, a white arrow indicating traffic flow around the roundabout.
Function: Informs of the upcoming roundabout, and directs on the correct path.

15. Crosswalk Sign

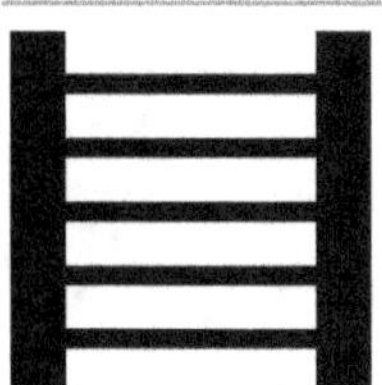

Rectangular sign, two white lines forming "X," pedestrian symbol.
Function: Indicates marked crosswalk, where pedestrians have the right of way, often near intersections.

16. No Right Turn on Red Sign

Circle sign, black arrow on white, signing "**NO RIGHT TURN**."

Function: Forbids right turns on red at the specified location, enhancing pedestrian safety.

17. Detour Sign

Rectangular sign, black arrow on orange background.

Function: Guides drivers around closures or construction. Follow detour signs for an alternative route, ensuring a smooth journey.

18. Merge Sign

Sign with two white arrows merging into one lane, often on yellow.

Function: Alerts drivers that two lanes are merging into one, encouraging smooth traffic flow and safe merging.

19. One Way Sign

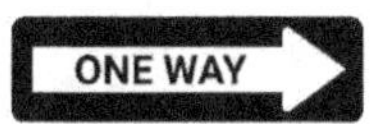

Rectangular sign, white arrow on black for one-way traffic.

Function: Informs drivers that the road is only accessible in the direction of the arrow.

20. Road Work Ahead Sign

Orange diamond with black symbols indicating road work.

Function: Warns drivers of upcoming road maintenance or construction. Expect reduced speed limits and potential lane closures.

21. Divided Highway Begins Sign

Diamond sign, yellow background, black symbols indicating a divided highway.

Function: Notifies drivers they're entering a section with a median or barrier separating opposing lanes.

22. Truck Crossing Sign

Yellow diamond with a black truck symbol.

Function: Alerts drivers to an upcoming intersection or area where trucks may be crossing.

23. Double Arrow Sign

Rectangular sign, two black arrows pointing in opposite directions.

Function: Indicates a reversible lane where traffic direction may change based on conditions or time of day.

24. Traffic Signal Ahead Sign

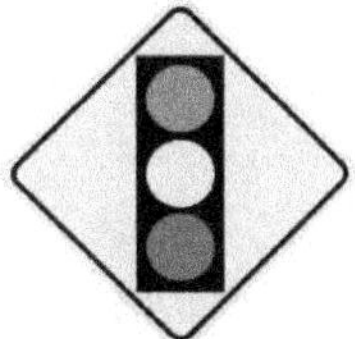

Rectangular sign, black traffic signal symbol on yellow.

Function: Informs drivers of an upcoming traffic signal. Prepare to adjust speed and follow signal instructions.

25. Lane Ends Merge Left Sign

Rectangular sign, white arrow merging left on orange.

Function: Notifies drivers that the lane is ending; merge left, commonly seen in construction zones.

26. School Bus Stop Ahead Sign

Yellow diamond with black school bus symbol and "AHEAD."

Function: Warns drivers of an upcoming school bus stop. Prepare to stop when the bus is loading or unloading children.

27. Watch for Wildlife Sign.

Rectangular sign with an animal symbol.

Function: Alerts drivers to possible wildlife crossing. Exercise caution and reduce speed in these areas.

28. Hazardous Materials Route Sign

Rectangular sign, white hazardous materials symbol on green.

Function: Designates routes for vehicles transporting hazardous materials. Drivers must follow specific regulations on these routes.

29. No Passing Zone Sign

Rectangular sign, yellow pennant symbolizes no passing.

Function: Marks areas where passing is prohibited due to limited visibility or potential hazards.

30. Advisory Speed Sign

Rectangular sign, the black arrow on a yellow background with advisory speed limit.
Function: Recommends a safe speed for curves, exits, or challenging road conditions.

31. Construction Zone Sign

Orange diamond-shaped signs and black symbols indicate construction equipment.

Function: Alerts drivers to an upcoming construction zone. Expect reduced speed limits, lane shifts, and possible detours.

32. No Parking Anytime Sign

Rectangular sign, red circle and slash over a parked car.

Function: Indicates areas where parking is prohibited at all times, often in busy urban areas.

33. Road Closed Sign

Rectangular sign, black barrier symbol, and "ROAD CLOSED."

Function: Informs drivers the road ahead is closed. Follow posted detour signs.

34. Deer Crossing Sign

Yellow diamond with black deer symbol.

Function: Warns of potential deer crossings. Exercise caution, especially during dawn and dusk. Drive attentively for wildlife safety.

35. Flashing Yellow Arrow Sign

Rectangular sign with a flashing yellow arrow.

Function: Indicates left turns allowed, but yield to oncoming traffic. Used at intersections with dedicated left-turn lanes.

36. No Horn Honking Zone Sign

Rectangular sign, horn symbol inside a red circle.

Function: Prohibits horn use within the designated area, often in residential neighborhoods.

37. . Right Lane Ends Sign

Rectangular sign, black arrow merging right on an orange background.
Function: Notifies drivers that the right lane is ending, and prepares to merge left.

38. Falling Rocks Sign

Yellow diamond-shaped sign, a black symbol of falling rocks.
Function: Warns of potential rockslides or falling debris. Exercise caution and be prepared for road hazards.

39. Roundabout Ahead Sign

Yellow circular sign, a black symbol indicating a roundabout.
Function: Alerts drivers to an upcoming roundabout. Prepare to navigate the circular intersection.

49. Bicycles May Use Full Lane Sign

Rectangular sign, "BICYCLES MAY USE FULL LANE."

Function: Informs drivers that bicycles may use the entire lane. Encourages safe sharing of the road.

42. Crosswind Sign

Rectangular sign, black wind lines on yellow background.

Function: Warns of potential crosswinds. Exercise caution, especially for high-profile vehicles.

42. Pavement Ends Sign

Rectangular sign with a symbol of pavement ending.

Function: Marks the end of a paved road. Prepare for a transition to a different road surface.

43. Truck Rollover Warning Sign

Rectangular sign with a black symbol of a tipped-over truck.

Function: Alerts drivers to the risk of truck rollovers, often on curves with advisory speeds.

44. Hill Sign

Rectangular sign with an icon indicating an upward or downward slope.
Function: Warns of an upcoming hill. Adjust speed accordingly for better control.

45. Hospital Sign

Rectangular sign with the word "**HOSPITAL**" and an arrow.
Function: Provides directional information to the nearest hospital or medical facility.

46. Merge Right Sign

Rectangular sign with a black arrow merging right on a yellow background.
Function: Indicates lane merging; drivers should prepare to merge to the right.

47. Road Narrows Sign

Rectangular sign with a black symbol of a narrowing road on a yellow background.
Function: Warns that the road ahead will narrow. Adjust speed and merge if necessary.

48. School Zone Speed Limit Sign

Rectangular sign with a yellow background indicating a reduced speed limit in a school zone.

Function: Informs drivers of the reduced speed limit when children are present near schools.

49. No Bicycles Allowed Sign

Circular sign with a red slash over a bicycle symbol.

Function: Prohibits bicycles from entering a designated area, such as a freeway or specific roadway.

59. Keep Right Sign

Rectangular sign with a black arrow pointing right on a yellow background.

Function: Reminds drivers to keep right of a traffic island, barrier, or other obstruction.

51. No Parking Fire Lane Sign

Function: Prohibits parking in fire lanes to ensure quick access for emergency vehicles.

52. Pedestrian Detour Sign

Rectangular sign with a pedestrian symbol and an arrow indicating a detour.

Function: Guides pedestrians around construction zones or areas where the sidewalk is inaccessible.

53. Reversible Lane Control Sign

Rectangular sign with black arrows indicating reversible lanes.

Function: Informs drivers of lanes that may change direction based on traffic conditions or time of day.

54. No Turn on Red Sign

Square sign with a red circle and slash over a right-turn arrow.

Function: Prohibits making a right turn on a red light at the specified location.

55. Service Signs (Gas, Food, Lodging)

Rectangular blue signs with symbols indicating services like gas, food, or lodging available at upcoming exits.

Function: Provides information about services at upcoming exits for drivers planning their stops.

56. Wrong Way Driver Sign

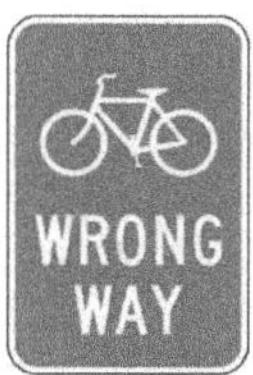

Rectangular sign with a white symbol of a vehicle facing the wrong direction on a red background.

Function: Warns drivers they are heading in the wrong direction, often placed on freeway ramps.

57. Tunnel Ahead Sign

Rectangular sign with a black tunnel entrance symbol on a yellow background.

Function: Warns of an upcoming tunnel. Exercise caution and follow posted speed limits.

58. Truck Escape Ramp Sign

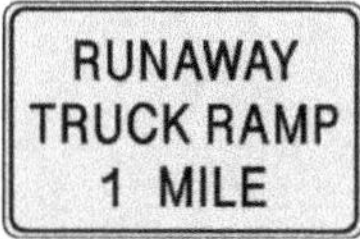

Rectangular sign with a black truck on an escape ramp symbol on a yellow background.

Function: Alerts truck drivers to an escape ramp ahead for emergencies, especially on downhill grades.

59. No Pedestrian Crossing Sign

Rectangular sign with a black pedestrian symbol in a red circle.

Function: Indicates areas where pedestrians cannot cross the road.

69. Slippery When Wet Sign

Rectangular sign with wavy lines indicating slipping on a wet road on a yellow background.

Function: Warns of slippery road conditions during wet weather. Exercise caution and reduce speed.

61. End School Zone Sign

A rectangular sign stating **"END SCHOOL ZONE."**

Function: Indicates the conclusion of a school zone with reduced speed limits. Resume normal speed for a safe journey.

62. Animal Crossing Sign

Rectangular sign with a black animal symbol on a yellow background.

Function: Alerts drivers to potential animal crossings. Exercise caution, especially in rural or wooded areas.

63. Two-Way Traffic Sign

Rectangular sign with symbols of two arrows indicating two-way traffic.

Function: Informs drivers they are entering a section with traffic flowing in both directions.

64. Crossbuck Railroad Crossing Sign

White X-shaped sign written"**RAILROAD CROSSING.**"

Function: Warns of an upcoming railroad crossing. Prioritize safety and yield to oncoming trains.

65. Handicap Parking Sign

Rectangular sign with the word "HANDICAP" and a wheelchair symbol.

Function: Designates parking for vehicles with handicap permits, ensuring accessibility.

Right-of-Way Rules

Understanding who moves first when **automobiles, pedestrians**, and **motorcycles** clash on the road is made simpler by obeying right-of-way restrictions. The right-of-way belongs to the first automobile to reach the intersection. Pedestrians, bicycles, and other automobiles must yield to the person having the right-of-way. You should never expect that other motorists will cede the right-of-way. When giving up your right-of-way may aid avert collisions, do so.

Intersection

Anywhere two roads converge is called an intersection. There are lights or signs at controlled intersections. Blind and uncontrolled intersections don't. Look left, right, and ahead before approaching a crossroads to make sure there are no automobiles, bicycles, or pedestrians close. Have the capacity to slow and stop when necessary. Pedestrians hold the right-of-way at all times. Here are a few rules regarding right-of-way at intersections:

Absent the **YIELD** or **STOP** signs: The right-of-way belongs to the first automobile to reach the intersection. On the other hand, you should surrender the right-of-way to individuals on your right if they arrive at the intersection at the same moment as you. This includes bikers and autos. When you reach a stop sign with one on each of the four

corners, stop first and follow the directions above.

T-intersections devoid of **YIELD** or **STOP** signage: On the through road (which continues straight ahead), automobiles, cyclists, and pedestrians have the right-of-way. When turning left, look out for pedestrians. Any pedestrian or incoming automobile that is close enough to be harmful should have the right-of-way.
When making a right turn, always watch out for persons crossing the street, as well as scooters and motorbikes moving alongside you.

Green light on the traffic signal Take caution as you travel. It is the right-of-way for pedestrians.
Starting a vehicle: You have to be careful when entering traffic and give way to cars that are already in the lanes. Stopping or blocking an intersection if there isn't enough clearance for everyone to cross before the traffic signal light turns red is prohibited.

Roundabout

- A central island is circled by traffic in a single direction in a roundabout.
- As you come near, slow down.
- Give way to every automobile that is presently on the circle.
- When there is ample room in the traffic to safely merge, enter on the right.
- Keep an eye out for guidance signs and lane markings.
- Rotate in the opposite direction of the clock. Don't stop or go by.
- When you combine or depart, offer a signal.
- If you happen to miss your exit, keep traveling until you locate it again.
- Select the entry or exit lane at the roundabout according to where you're heading if there are numerous lanes available.

The image below shows this.

Turn right (yellow car)

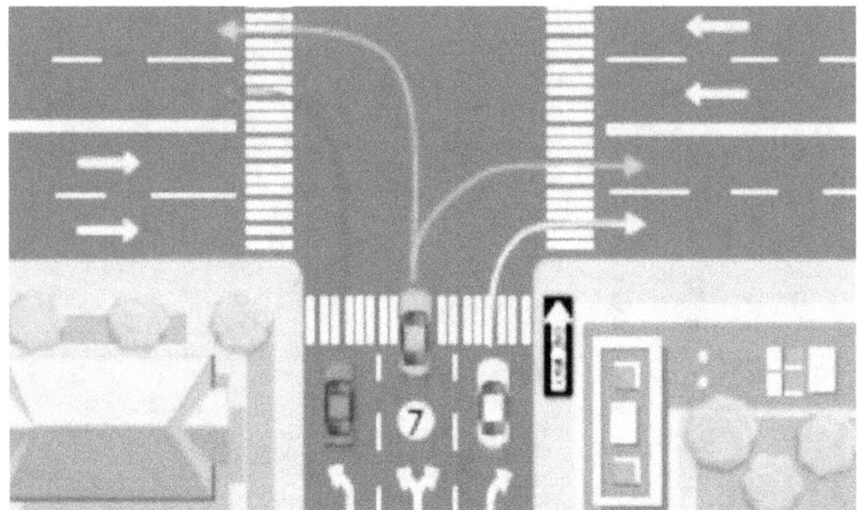

Select the proper lane and get out of it.
Proceed straight (red car) and select any lane. Take the lane you entered to depart.

Turn left

Go ahead and take the specified exit by driving until you arrive there.
Yes, Make a Straight Left to Invert People on foot
These are classified as vulnerable road users or pedestrians: a person on foot.
a person who is not riding a bicycle or driving a vehicle. This includes a skateboard, roller skates, etc.

- A handicapped person traveling around on a wheelchair, tricycle, or quadricycle.
- Tricycle, quadricycle, normal wheelchair, and electric wheelchair, from left to right.
- Pedestrians have the right-of-way, but they also have to adhere to traffic regulations.
- Whether there is a crosswalk or not, you have to drive cautiously, slow down, or stop when a pedestrian is crossing the roadway so they may cross safely.

factors are:
- When an automobile is stopped at a crosswalk, do not pass it. It's conceivable that you won't spot a pedestrian crossing the road.
- A pedestrian is preparing to cross the street if they gaze up at you. Give way to the pedestrian.

- It is crucial to always allow pedestrians ample time to cross the roadway safely. Certain populations, like the elderly, parents of small children, and those with disabilities, may require additional time.

Crosswalks

The section of the road allocated for people to cross it safely is called a crosswalk. Usually, white lines are used to denote them. There may be yellow crosswalk lines at school crossings. Not every crossing has markers.

In crosswalks that are either marked or unmarked, pedestrians have the right of way. Stop at the limit line and allow pedestrians to cross the street if there is one before the crosswalk.

A few crosswalks contain lights that flash. Keep an eye out for pedestrians and be ready to stop whether or not the lights are flashing.

People Walking with Blindness

- At all times, pedestrians who are using white canes or guide dogs have the right-of-way. These pedestrians may be blind in one or both eyes. When turning or backing up, exercise care. This is particularly critical if you are running an electric or hybrid automobile since blind pedestrians rely on sound to identify the presence of impending traffic.
- In the middle of a crossing, never stop. A blind person may be pushed by this to cross the street outside of the crosswalk.
- Never honk your horn at someone who is blind.

- When a visually challenged person retracts their cane and steps away from the junction, it often signifies that you are free to depart.

Roads in the Mountains

When two automobiles meet on a tiny, steep road and neither can pass, the car facing uphill is entitled to the right-of-way. When backing up a slope, the automobile that is facing downwards has better control. When an uphill automobile seeks to pass, the downhill vehicle must surrender.

Lane Usage and Markings

Lanes for traffic

A piece of road designated for one line of traffic is called a traffic lane.

Lane Signage

Road surfaces with lane markings make it easier for drivers to comprehend traffic laws and which portion of the road to utilize.

One Yellow Line That Is Solid

On a road with two-way traffic, the center is indicated by a single, solid yellow line. If there is just one lane of traffic moving in your direction and a strong yellow line on your side of the road, you should not overtake the car in front of you.

Two Solid Yellow Lines in Double

Avoid crossing across twice-solid yellow lines. Unless you are: stay to the right of these lines.
in a carpool lane reserved for high-occupancy vehicles (HOVs), with an entrance on the left.

directed to drive on the other side of the road because your side is closed off or obstructed by construction or other signage.

- doing a U-turn or turning left over a single set of double yellow lines to access or depart a driveway or private road.
- A barrier consists of two sets of solid double yellow lines that are separated by at least two feet. Except in specified openings, do not drive on, over, or execute a left turn over this barrier.

Broken Yellow Line

If a broken yellow line is next to your driving lane, you are allowed to pass. Pass only when it's secure.

one solid white line

Traffic lanes traveling in the same direction are indicated by a single, solid white line. This also applies to one-way streets.

Two Solid White Lines

A lane barrier that separates a preferred use lane, such as a carpool (HOV) lane, from a normal use lane is indicated by two solid white lines. Double solid white lines may also be seen in or close to highways on/off ramps. Never cross two solid white lines to change lanes. Hold off until

only one white line breaks

➤ White lines that are broken

On roadways with two or more lanes going in the same direction, traffic lanes are separated by broken white lines.

Lane-end markers

Large broken lines are often used to indicate the end of street and highway lanes. Be ready to get off the highway or wait for the lane to terminate if you are traveling in one that has broken lines in it. Seek for a sign instructing you to combine or get out.

Line of Yield, A yield line is a triangle-shaped, solid white line that instructs oncoming cars when to stop or yield. The triangles indicate the direction of oncoming cars.

Selecting a Lane

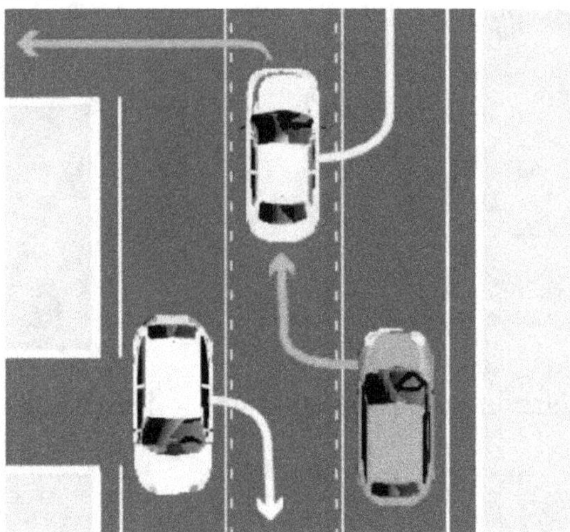

It's common to refer to traffic lanes by numbers. The Number 1 Lane is the left (or fast) lane. The Number 2 Lane is the one that is located to the right of the Number 1 Lane. Then the Lane with Number 3, etc.

➤ The following advice may help you choose a lane:
  - Turn left or use the left lane to pass.
  - When you enter or leave traffic, or when you come onto the road from a shoulder or curb, stay in the right lane.

Changing Directions

➤ Before lane switching:

- Give a signal.
- Examine the mirrors in your room.
- Examine the traffic next to and behind you.
- Make sure the lane is free by looking over your shoulder in the direction you want to go.
- Look out for bicycles, motorcyclists, and other vehicles in your blind zones. Keep the car from straying into another lane.
- Verify that there is enough room for your car in the next lane. Before a lane change, there is no need to reduce your speed.
- Try to keep to one lane at all times. Avoid dodging and weaving across traffic. Accident risk may rise with last-minute lane or direction changes. Continue forward after you have crossed an intersection. Make sure you finish any turns that you begin. Continue driving if you miss a turn until you can do it legally and safely.

Lane Types

➢ Lanes of Passage

The passing lane, also known as the far left lane, is the one that is closest to the center divider on a multilane road and is where cars pass one another.

➢ High-occupancy vehicle (HOV) and carpool lanes

Carpools, buses, motorcyclists, and low-emission cars with stickers are all permitted to utilize HOV lanes. If one of these applies, you may utilize an HOV lane:

There are a certain number of people in your car. The minimal number of persons will be indicated by signage at the on-ramp or along the route. Also, road signage indicates which hours are subject to the HOV regulations.

You are operating a car with zero or low emissions. You have to wear a unique decal provided by the DMV.

You are (unless otherwise indicated) a motorcyclist.

A diamond emblem with the words "Carpool Lane" designates the road surface in an HOV lane. When entering or leaving an HOV lane, never pass over two solid lines. Make use of the specified exits and entrances.

Turn lanes on the center-left

A two-way roadway has a center left turn lane in the middle of it. Two painted lines designate it on both sides. The outside line is solid, whereas the inner line is broken. To get ready for and execute a left turn or U-turn, use the middle left turn lane. It isn't a typical passing or traffic lane. Only 200 feet may be traveled in the middle left turn lane. From this lane, turn left:

Keep an eye out for oncoming traffic in the center left turn lane.

- Give a signal.
- Look over your shoulder to see where you are blind.
- Make a full merge into the center left turn lane to avoid obstructing traffic.
- When it's safe, turn.

Lanes or Turnout Spaces

There are designated pullout areas or lanes on several two-lane roadways. To make room for vehicles behind you to pass, merge into these lanes or locations.

When you are traveling slowly on a two-lane road and there are five or more cars behind you, you must utilize a pullout area or lane to allow other vehicles to pass.

- Makes a Left Turn
- Turning to the left:
- Move into the left turn lane or very near the center separator.
- Turn left into the designated turn lane at the entrance. Don't cross any solid lines.
- Enter a two-way center left turn lane 200 feet before the turn. Remember to give way to any incoming traffic, including bicycles and motorcyclists. At all times, give way to pedestrians.
- Start your signal one hundred feet before the turn.
- Gently slow down and check over your left shoulder.
- Stay behind the perimeter. If there's no limit line, you should stop before you enter the crossing. If there isn't a crossing, you should stop before you get to the intersection.
- When it's safe to do so, take a left, right, and left glance before beginning your turn.
- Proceed into the intersection after completing your turn in the left lane.
- Refrain from changing into the oncoming car's lane by not turning the wheel too rapidly.
- Until it's safe to begin your turn, keep your wheels facing straight ahead. You run the risk of being flung into oncoming traffic if you are driving with your wheels facing left and a car hits you from behind.
- When you come around the bend, gradually increase your pace.
- In the new lane, let the steering wheel straighten.
- Turn to the left when the light turns red.

- Turning left against the red light is allowed when entering a one-way street from another. Make sure that no signs are preventing you from making the turn. Bicycles with green lights, pedestrians, and approaching cars must yield. Look in both directions while turning is safe.

U-turns

Turning around and going back to the original route is known as a U-turn. Signal and use the far-left or left turn lane to do a U-turn. Turn around by going through the two yellow lines.

if you are in a neighborhood and no automobile is in sight for 200 feet.

- At a junction where there is a green light or green arrow, there is a visible no-turn sign if the split road has a central divider opening.
- Where a "No U-turn" sign is posted, you should never turn around.
- inside or near an overpass for trains.
- by crossing two sets of double yellow lines on a divided roadway, a curb, a strip of land, or a dividing portion.

when you can't see well for 200 feet in any direction according to a single file before the fire station. In the driveway of a fire station, never turn around.

Business districts are the parts of towns and cities where most offices and companies are situated.

The explanations that follow refer to the Turns Number illustrations that are next to the automobiles in the photographs. Between your automobile and the curb, keep an eye out for motorcycles, bicycles, and pedestrians. When making turns, there may be signs or indications that suggest you may exit or turn from more than one lane.

Turn left off of a two-way street.

1.Start the turn in the left-hand lane closest to the road's center. To reduce the likelihood of an accident, complete the turn in the left lane that is closest to the center of the road while driving in the direction of your vehicle.

2. Turn to the right. Turning should begin and end in the lane closest to the right border of the road. Refrain from veering into the path of approaching vehicles.

3. After exiting a two-way street, turn left into a one-way street. Start the turn in the lane that is farthest from the center of the road, on the far left. If there are three or more lanes in the direction you are going, you may finish your turn in any free lane.

4. Turn left into a two-way street after crossing a one-way street. Take the far-left lane to initiate the turn. To reduce the likelihood of an accident, complete the turn in the left lane that is closest to the center of the road while driving in the direction of your vehicle.

5. Making a left turn into a one-way street after exiting another one. Take the far-left lane to initiate the turn. It is permitted for bikes to turn left in the left turn lane. If there are three or more lanes in the direction you are going, you may finish your turn in any free lane.

6. Making a right turn into a one-way street after leaving one. Make the turn in the lane to the far right. You may exit the turn in any lane if it's safe to do so.

7. Make a left turn into a two-way street at a "T" junction from a one-way street. The right-of-way is granted to traffic traveling directly through the intersection. From the center lane, you may turn left or right.

Braking

- Remove your foot off the gas pedal (accelerator) and let the automobile slow down. Lightly press the brake until you come to a full stop. Give yourself adequate room and time to create this method.
- When halted at a limit line, do not cross over the line. If stopping behind a vehicle, leave an adequate distance to observe the rear wheels.

Merging And Exiting

➢ Merging

Highway traffic has the right-of-way, You must stay in the right lane on the on-ramp when you enter a highway.

- Follow or maintain the speed of the traffic.
- Turn onto the roadway when it is safe to do so. Continue until you are completely

essential.

- Merge into a space wide enough for your automobile to safely join the lane.
- Make use of your turn signals and mirrors.

- Before changing lanes or swerving into oncoming traffic, swiftly swivel your head to peek over your shoulder.
- Allow three seconds between your automobile and the one in front of you to guarantee a safe stop.

NOTE: When merging, avoid traveling over any solid lines. Give way and cross each lane one at a time if you need to cross numerous lanes. Every time you travel, examine your blind zones for automobiles, motorcycles, bicycles, and pedestrians.

➢ Exiting

To safely get off a highway

- Recognize when your exit is approaching and know where it is.
- Should you desire to swap lanes, go one at a time. To check your blind spots, signal and turn to look over your shoulder.
- Give a signal five seconds (or roughly 400 feet) before you exit the designated lane.
- Make sure you're departing at a safe rate.
- When departing, avoid walking over any solid lines Getting into or out of traffic
- allow way to incoming traffic and allow yourself ample space to come up to the speed of the oncoming car. You require a space that combines, enters, or departs traffic.
- On city streets, half a block is roughly 150 feet.
- On the highway, a complete block is roughly 300 feet.
- If people or automobiles are blocking your way, do not cross the intersection, even if you have the green light.

NOTE: When making a left turn, never expect that an automobile approaching you with its right turn signal on will turn before it gets to you. The automobile may have mistakenly switched on its signal or be ready to go right past you. Before making the left turn, wait for the automobile to start its turn.

➢ Going Away

Every time you approach nearby, you have to determine if you have enough space to pass, A cyclist or an incoming automobile.

- a barrier, curve, hill, or crossroads. The slope or curve needs to be at least 1/3 of a mile distant to be safely passed.
- Look ahead for any conditions on the road that might force other automobiles to swerve into your lane before you pass.

- Don't succeed: if you are going to enter a bend or a hill and are unable to observe whether any other cars are close. On single- and double-lane roads, this is highly perilous.
- within 100 feet of a railroad crossing, bridge, tunnel, junction, or other potentially hazardous place.

Sharing the Road with Other Vehicles

Let's face it, we don't always know what to do (or not do) when it comes to sharing the road with others. Anyone who has tried to pass an 18-wheeler or been behind a slow-moving automobile would know.

Here's a basic explanation of the regulations regarding sharing the road with trucks, buses, motorcyclists, bicycles, slow-moving automobiles, and pedestrians. There's also a message about how crucial it is to yield to emergency vehicles.

Vehicles

As stated by the Federal Motor Carrier Safety Administration, a huge rig may weigh up to twenty or thirty times as much as a regular vehicle. Their great height and weight hinder their ability to stop, move, and navigate maneuvers and lane changes swiftly. Trucks have enormous blind zones even with mirrors and a bird's eye view. And the truck driver probably doesn't even realize you're there if your car is in one.

Drive into the empty spot right in front of the truck to avoid cutting them off. When a fully laden commercial vehicle moves at the same velocity as a conventional passenger car, it takes twice as long to stop (about 300 feet). The car may not be able to slow down and avert an accident if you're too close.

Never try to avoid a truck to turn or get to an exit. Remain behind and slow down.

Recognize and keep clear of a truck's blind spots. These are frequently on the sides, notably the right side, and directly in front of and behind. Generally speaking, you may infer that a truck driver cannot see you if you are unable to see his or her picture in the side mirror.

The turning path will be bigger for longer trucks. When turning, large rig drivers typically swing wide. That is, executing a rapid left turn before making a right turn. Keep an eye on the truck driver's turn lights and expect a reversal of course. Most essential, avoid getting in the path of a truck when turning by not passing one.

When passing a truck, always keep to the left. Don't remain after you've gone. To let the car know you are there, walk ahead of it.

Avoid tailgating. If the truck in front of you stops quickly, you may not have enough time to stop.

Buses

Many of the same problems with stopping and maneuvering that affect trucks also affect buses. In addition, the driver must carry the duty of a big group of passengers, including occasionally small ones. There are additional elements to take into mind when driving next to a bus, such as frequent stops and people getting on and off.

There are warning lights on school buses. Flashing red denotes stop, whereas flashing yellow signals slow down. No matter where your automobile is, even if it is close to the bus, you must stop.

Keep in mind that passing a school bus that has stopped to pick up or drop off kids is against the law.

Expect several stops from public buses as well. Keep your distance securely behind them.

Buses and other big vehicles must move more slowly around curves and on-ramps owing to their larger center of gravity. Modify your speed if you're lagging behind them. Don't unplug them.

Recall that, like trucks, buses also have wide blind zones. Usually, they are located directly behind the rear bumper and the side flat mirrors. Stay conspicuous and keep away from such areas.

Motorcycles

Motorcycles are substantially smaller than trucks and buses, as well as smaller than vehicles. Thus, it's clear how they may nearly "disappear" in your peripheral vision. Motorcycles could emerge abruptly and you may not even notice them. Because of this, you should continuously be extremely careful and alert of any vehicle that is sharing the road with you.

- When you change lanes, move onto a major highway, or undertake a visual examination, make use of your mirrors.
- When it is practical, offer motorcyclists the complete lane width.
- A motorcycle that is in the same lane as you should never be tried to pass. Give them room to pass by shifting to one side.
- Motorcyclists may suddenly shift their speed or direction according to road circumstances. These include potholes, gravel, and moist, slippery surfaces. Be prepared to shift your lane and speed in preparation for this.
- Before opening your car door after parking, examine the area for motorcyclists.

bicycles

As long as they are respecting the regulations, bicycles are permitted to travel on the road alongside other automobiles. This means riding in the direction of traffic, using reflectors and suitable lighting at night, signaling lane changes, and striving to maintain as near to the right curb as practical. There may occasionally be a dedicated bike lane for cyclists.

Be informed that in rare circumstances, if there is no approved alternative route and no signs banning riding, bicycles may be permitted to ride on some highway segments.

Bike turn signals are the same as for automobiles. The left arm extended to the side denotes a left turn. The left arm is bent at a ninety-degree angle and the hand is at the top when performing a right turn. With the hand at the bottom, the stop signal is the same. Acquire skill in hand signals to interpret the message provided by the rider.

Keep in mind that a bike may weigh as little as 20 pounds, but your car might weigh up to 20 tons. A rider and their bike can experience severe injury from your car.

There are restrictions in numerous countries controlling how much space you have to provide bicyclists. Generally speaking, you should leave them three feet of room.

NOTE: Check before you open your car door after parking. A bike could be on its way.

Slow-Going Automobiles

Being backed up by road maintenance vehicles, farm tractors, or carts hauled by animals may be frustrating. Usually, these slow-moving automobiles will have an orange triangle that reflects light on them so you can determine how rapidly they are approaching you.

- Decelerate Before you arrive at the slow-moving automobile, drop your speed.
- Avoid blaring your horn. Squealing your horn will not help a slow-moving car move any faster, and you risk frightening a horse.
- Animal-powered vehicles may move unexpectedly, so be careful.
- Move gently to the left to pass them if there is ample room.

Pedestrians

Pedestrians and automobiles regularly share the road when crossing the street. This would normally occur at a crossing. Verify the laws in your region. Pedestrians may not always have the right of way in certain instances. Nonetheless, to avoid striking pedestrians, drivers do need to pay attention to them.

- At any crossroads where people are waiting to cross, halt, Ensure that your car is five feet or less from the crossing. This makes your automobile more conspicuous to blind pedestrians.
- Never turn without first looking for pedestrians.
- When there is low vision, like at night, in darkness, or severe weather, proceed with extra caution. A pedestrian who is not visible to you might exist.
- Never drive past a vehicle that is stopped at a crosswalk. They might be coming to a standstill for someone.
- Make room. Imagine an emergency braking system for a vehicle that can distinguish bikes and pedestrians.

Emergency Automobiles

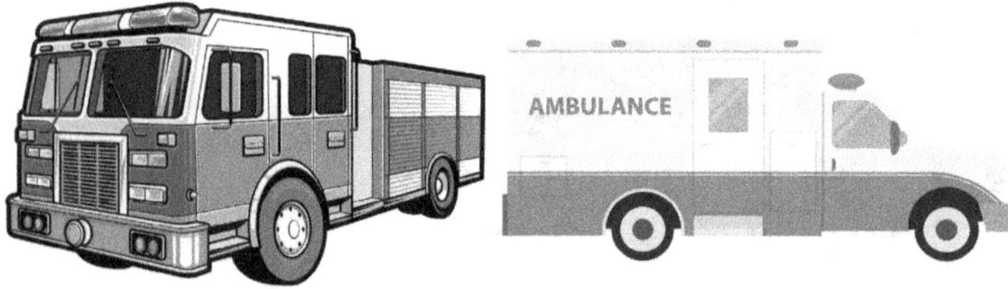

Ambulances, fire engines, and police cars must arrive at the sites where they can help persons in need. It's time to pull over to the side of the road when you see flashing lights or hear sirens. Providing emergency vehicles with a clear path to their location can be useful.

You may help yourself remain safe by sticking to these traffic-sharing recommendations. Should you require such coverage, having the right automobile insurance policy will bring you peace of mind. Travel safely.

Chapter 3: Safe Driving Practices

Defensive Driving Techniques

Thinking ahead is a must for all drivers For RV drivers, Defensive is even more important than it is for drivers of passenger automobiles. Since directional changes are slower and the RV needs more clearance in traffic, an RV driver must always be aware of the traffic around them. Aim to stay off the roads when traffic is heavy Ask someone, maybe a passenger, for help finding your route if you are driving in an unfamiliar region, and make sure you always have a map with you. When driving alone, be sure to stop the vehicle and pull over in a safe spot before checking a map.

Wherever you are going, tune in to the local radio stations. Watch out for accidents, slowdowns in traffic, road work, etc. With a map in hand and little preparation, you may choose many paths.

Getting Started and Changing To minimize wear and pressure on the hitch and transmission systems, always aim for a smooth start and shift (for manual transmissions). Shifting Trends

Your turning patterns must be adjusted for longer wheelbases. At intersections, you have to veer wider to avoid having the rear wheel roll over the curb. To increase the turning radius, move your lane position and go farther into the intersection before starting the turn.

Roadway curves may sometimes be difficult to navigate. When making a right turn, stay close to the center of the lane to prevent the rear wheels from coming off the pavement. Stay to the right of the lane while making a left bend or curve to prevent the trailer's tail from tracking into the oncoming traffic lane.

Because of their high centers of gravity, RVs and certain trailers need to be driven more slowly while navigating curves and turns to avoid swaying. Before you get to the turn, slow down.

Be careful while transporting livestock since they could shift around in a trailer. This shifts the center of gravity and increases the likelihood of a rollover. When carrying less than a full load of cattle, use barriers to maintain the herd's unity. Still, use considerable caution while navigating curves. Additionally, livestock may lean while bending, which might result in a rollover if you are moving too quickly.

Winds

Exercise extreme care while driving in windy conditions. Crosswinds are the largest threat because, if you're not ready, they may force a large mobile home or a vehicle and trailer combo into another lane. This is especially valid for travel trailers. The best defense against strong winds is to move more slowly in most situations. When pulling a trailer, you should use the trailer brakes gradually to help steady a trailer that is wobbling. A heavier throttle is required in headwinds to maintain regular speeds. In strong gusts, you may be able to drive an RV, but it would be safer to pull over and wait it out. If you want to travel in areas with high winds, find out the local weather and road conditions by getting in touch with someone. Local airports, the Highway Patrol, the State Police, and ranger stations are excellent sources of weather information. There are often signs along the route that provide radio frequencies for meteorological data.

When traveling through a snowy area, always carry the driving wheel and trailer wheel chains. Understand how to wear them. Both the tow vehicle and one of the trailer's axles need chains. You will need chains for one tire on each side if your motor home has twin rear wheels.
Freeze

When towing a trailer on icy roads, proceed cautiously, especially when going downhill. Employ the lower gears. It could be possible to increase the tow vehicle's traction by gradually loosening the load equalizing the hitch's tension. When the ice road scenario has passed, always reset the hitch since regular driving circumstances may cause the vehicle to lose stability.

Roads in the Mountains

Will your vehicle pass muster? Regardless matter how bad they are, almost all grades will cause you to slow down. More than six percent of an elevation is deemed serious and requires special attention. You will need to use lower gears more to climb hills or mountains the higher the gradient, the longer the slope, and the heavier the load.

Gravity will usually accelerate you while you're going down a steep hill. Choose a low gear, apply enough brake pressure to hold you back without letting the brakes become too hot, and maintain an appropriate safe pace. Utilize the engine's braking action (lower gears) as your primary speed management strategy to save your brakes and enable you to slow down or stop as required by the road and traffic conditions. Before descending a steep, slow down the vehicle and shift the transmission into a low gear.

Remember that using the brakes during a long and/or steep descent is only an addition to the engine's braking action. The following is a good braking strategy after the vehicle is in the appropriate low gear:

1. Only apply enough force to the brakes to cause a noticeable slowdown.
2. Release the brakes after you've reduced your speed to around five mph below your "safe" pace. This application of brake pressure should last for around three seconds.

Once you reach your "safe" speed, go back and repeat steps 1 and 2.

When driving on a multiple-lane slope, avoid using the fast lanes. If your RV or trailer is not going to stay below the posted speed limit, stay in the far right lane while going up a steep slope. Rather than trying to pass slow-moving cars and jam up the faster lanes because you don't have enough power, it would be smarter to shift into a lower gear and slow down.

Small Roads

Some two-lane roads have designated "turn-out" areas. You may drive into these spaces and give oncoming traffic room to pass. A passing lane is a characteristic of several two-lane roads. To allow faster automobiles to pass you in the passing lane, stay in the right lane. If you are driving a slow automobile on a two-lane highway or a route where passing is difficult and there are five or more cars behind you, you should pull over to the side of the road as soon as it is safe to do so to give them space to pass.

To allow the vehicles behind you to see ahead, try to stay to the right of the lane. Always remember to yield to faster vehicles and get off the road when it is safe to do so.

Escape Ramps: Designed to safely halt rogue cars without harming drivers or passengers, escape ramps have been installed on several steep mountain slopes. Escape ramps, often used in conjunction with an upgrade, use a long bed of loose, soft material (sand or pea gravel) to slow down a straying car.

Recognize the locations of any escape ramps along your path. Road signs indicate to drivers the locations of ramps.

Road Signs

Observe traffic signals alerting you to the dangers of driving a vehicle with a trailer. Could you turn your automobile around if you missed the notice warning of a "Dead End" ahead? What was the weight limit for the next bridge? Have you noticed the overpass's height clearance? Since you've never had to be concerned about these kinds of signs in your passenger vehicle, you may not be able to notice them. In your RV, you will have to worry about them.

Driving on Freeways

As you go closer to a highway, your acceleration will be slower, therefore you'll need more space. Keep in mind that vehicles traveling on highways have the right-of-way, so you must look for gaps large enough to accommodate your car or vehicles. Additionally, you need more space to pass other cars. It takes talent to estimate how much space you will demand. You may have to quickly swerve into another lane if you don't give yourself enough space and time to make a move. A trailer may slide, oversteer, swing, or fishtail as a consequence of this.

Since you are unable to stop your automobile quickly, you must also increase the following distances. Reduce your speed earlier than you would in a smaller vehicle when you want to exit a highway. Remember that a lot of off-ramps have curves that become tighter with time. To prevent the rear wheels from scraping the curb or coming off the pavement, you must stay on the outside of the turn.

Cars towing trailers are required by law (CVC §22406) to stay in the right-hand traffic lane or as close to the curb or right edge as is reasonably possible. You may drive in the lane immediately to the left of the right-hand traffic lane on a split highway where there are four or more lanes of traffic traveling in the same direction, or when a specific lane or lanes are not designated. When passing or moving ahead of another car traveling in the same direction, you have to employ one of the following: The right-hand traffic lane when using it is permitted, the designated lane, or the lane immediately to the left of the right-hand lane.

Unpaved or dirt roads

There are sometimes occasions when a dirt or gravel road is the only way into the campground. To find out whether a certain route is suitable for your vehicle, check out a database of campsites. Take careful note of and trust the indications that are offered. Avoid using a road if there is a notice prohibiting trailers. A four-wheel drive vehicle is the only one equipped to handle potential hazards like washed-out sections of the road, low trees, or rocks that may lie ahead.

Vacation Travel

Making adequate preparations might reduce the majority of the traffic over the holidays. A lot of campsites take reservations. You may want to consider taking a different route since the roadways that go to several well-known locations might become congested. It's a good idea to arrive early in the day if you haven't booked reservations since both private and municipal campgrounds fill up quickly. Get some good sleep the night before.

It's not as easy as it seems to drive. Every two to three hours, take a 15- to 30-minute break from driving to help you stay refreshed. Step out of your automobile and take a walk about. This will help to relax weary eyes and loosen up tense muscles. Take this chance to inspect your vehicle. It will also increase your level of focus.

REMEMBER: Because the body naturally wants to sleep at night, night driving may be especially dangerous. At night, especially after midnight, most drivers are less alert. The only safe course of action if you're feeling sleepy is to get off the road and get some rest. You endanger not only your own life but also the lives of others if you don't.

Handling Various Road Conditions

1. Winter roads need extra caution. As the temperature decreases, be ready for ice conditions. Put snow tires on your vehicles and make sure you have ice scrapers and snow chains on you. Take into account the road conditions and modify your speed to accommodate longer stopping distances.

2. Roadways may become slick after rain. Make sure your tires have enough wear, and turn on your headlights to improve visibility. Maintain a safe following distance since slippery roads might cause skidding if you brake suddenly. Make good use of the windshield wipers to keep your vision clean.

3. Going out onto dirt or gravel roads calls for another strategy. To keep control, slow down and use caution while making corners to avoid skidding. To get more traction, switch on the four-wheel drive on your car. To guarantee optimum performance on uneven terrain, check the tire pressure regularly.

4. With numerous stops and starts as well as erratic traffic patterns, driving in cities has special obstacles. Remain focused, make good use of mirrors, and foresee any impediments. Select routes with the least amount of traffic, and use navigation applications to get real-time traffic information.

5. Mountain roads may be narrow and steep, requiring cautious driving. To prevent brakes from overheating and to keep your speed constant while descending, downshift. Changes in altitude may have an impact on your car and your health, so pay attention to them.

6. Because fog obscures vision, greater vigilance is required. Avoid driving at high speeds and use your low-beam headlights. If visibility is really poor, pull over safely and wait for things to get better. Keep an ear out for any sounds of traffic and go forward with caution.

7. You must move more slowly and with more awareness while you are in a construction zone. Observe signs, abide by established speed restrictions, and be ready for unexpected lane changes. Keep a safe distance from construction equipment since there could be workers around.

8. Long, solitary expanses and intense heat are problems seen in desert terrain. Make sure your car has regular maintenance to avoid malfunctions. Always have enough water with you, and pay attention to temperature changes, particularly at night.

NOTE: Your best friends when it comes to managing different road conditions are flexibility and readiness. By being aware of the distinct difficulties that each situation offers, you can turn the trip into a smooth adventure that guarantees your safety and happiness on the many routes that open up in front of you.

Navigating Intersections and Roundabouts

How to Handle Roundabouts

First Step 1:
- Slow down as you get closer to the roundabout.
- Pay attention to oncoming cars in the roundabout as well as people using the crosswalks.

Step 2:
- Plan your escape route before you get in.
- If you want to proceed straight or make a right exit, stay in the right lane.
- If you want to travel straight, do a U-turn, or make a left turn, use the left lane.

Step 3:

- A safe space in the flow of traffic should exist before you enter.
- Give way to cars that are already on the roundabout; they are entitled to it.

Step 4:

- Once a secure opening appears, proceed to enter the roundabout.
- Within the roundabout, stay to the right and pay attention to how the road curves.

Step 5:

- Stay in your designated lane while navigating the roundabout.
- It is forbidden to switch lanes inside a roundabout.

Step 6:

- Keep an eye out for those using the designated crosswalks to cross the roundabout.
- Give way to pedestrians; they are entitled to the right of way.

Step 7:

- Indicate that you plan to leave before you get to the place you want to.
- When turning, use your left turn signal for a left turn and your right turn signal for a right.

Step 8:

- Carefully exit the roundabout, keeping an eye out for other cars and pedestrians.
- Refrain from stopping within the roundabout unless necessary due to traffic circumstances.

Step 9:

- When you see an emergency vehicle arriving, pull off of the roundabout and to the right.

Step 10:

- Recognize that other drivers may not adhere to the traffic laws.
- Remain alert and modify your position and pace as necessary.

Handling intersection

- Slow down as you get closer to the junction.
- Look for road markings, traffic signs, and signals that indicate the laws of the junction.
- Pay attention to yield, stop, and traffic signal signs.
- Recognize when someone has the right of way and obey any signs that are flashed.
- Determine if the junction is controlled, uncontrolled, circular, etc.
- Take into account the kind of junction when predicting other drivers' behavior.
- Look for people walking at crosswalks.
- Be mindful of other bicycles that could be using the road.
- Depending on where you want to go, park your car in the proper lane.
- Give other vehicles plenty of notice of your intentions by using turn signals.
- Keep an eye out for cars that are about to make a turn.
- Watch out for left-hand turns made by approaching vehicles.
- Maintain a safe following distance, giving yourself enough leeway to respond to unexpected   changes in the vehicle in front.
- If there isn't enough room on the opposite side of a junction, stay away from it.
- Keep looking left, right, and forward.
- Pay attention to blind areas, particularly while changing lanes or turning.
- Be ready to stop at a stop sign or whenever the traffic signal changes.
- When a car or pedestrian has the right of way, yield to them.
- As soon as it is safe to do so, take immediate action to clear the junction.
- Avert impeding other lanes or crosswalks.
- Even after you've left the junction, keep an eye out for any possible threats.
- Modify speed to correspond with traffic flow.

Essential Parking Rules and Tips

parallel Parking

Parking parallel to the road and other parked automobiles is known as parallel parking. To parallel park:

1. Locate a room. Find a location that is at least three feet longer than your automobile. Turn on your signal to indicate that you plan to park when you identify a location.

2. Approach the automobile in front of the area from the side. Give the automobile next to you a distance of roughly two feet. When your rear bumper lines up with the front of your parking location, stop. Continue to utilize your signal.

3. Examine your regions of blindness. Keep an eye out for incoming automobiles and pedestrians by monitoring your rearview mirror and your shoulder.

4. Start abstaining. A 45-degree angle should be produced when you spin the steering wheel to reverse into the region.

5. Make amends. When your rear wheel is within eighteen inches of the curb, start rotating the steering wheel away from it. To straighten out, you may have to pull both forward and backward. Right now, your automobile should be parallel to the curb and only 18 inches away from it.

6. Parking. After shutting off your automobile, activate the parking brake. Be cautious to check the area for passing vehicles, motorcycles, and motorbikes before stepping out of your automobile. When it's safe to go, do so.

Linear Supporting

To withdraw straight ahead: traffic analysis. Keep an eye on traffic and search for any relevant blind spots.

Give a signal. Turn on the turn signal before you reach the curb. Once done, shut off the turn signal.

Examine your regions of blindness. Keep an eye out for incoming automobiles and pedestrians by monitoring your rearview mirror and your shoulder.

Start retreating. Remaining three feet from the curb, return in a straight line for three vehicle lengths. When backing up, pay attention to what's behind you.

Mastery. Reverse at a steady, safe rate and adjust the steering wheel as required to retain control of the automobile. Work on keeping the vehicle straight until you can. To walk away from the curb, repeat steps 1 and 2.

Parking Uphill

- Wheels near the curb when sliding downward.
- Turn the wheels away from the curb when traveling uphill.
- No curb: shift the wheels in the direction of the road's shoulder.

A mechanical issue could cause your automobile to slip when you park on a hill. Don't forget to activate the parking brake and park the car or, if you have a manual transmission, put it in the drive. To draw up:

When driving on a sloping driveway, put the vehicle in park, apply the parking brake, and then spin the wheels to prevent it from rolling into the street.

> **Heading downhill:** Shift your front wheels right toward the roadside or into the curb.
> **Heading uphill**: Allow your vehicle to roll back a few inches by rotating your front wheels away from the curb and left toward the center of the road. The wheel and curb should make gentle contact.

Without a curb, traveling either uphill or downhill: If the brakes fail, spin the wheels so the vehicle will roll away from the center of the road.

At the colored curbs, parking

Parking laws are different for painted-colored curbs.

White: Just make quick trips to pick up and drop off folks.

Green: Let the vehicle idle for a time. The time limit could be inscribed on the curb or posted on signs.

Yellow: Pack and unpack freight and people. Don't stop past the required period. You must generally stay in your automobile if you drive a noncommercial vehicle.

Red: No parking, no pausing, no standing. A red zone designated for buses alone is where buses may stop.

Blue: Parking allocated for handicapped individuals or for drivers of disabled persons who are displaying special license plates or placards.

Parking Illegally

Wherever a No Parking sign is posted, you should never park or leave your automobile either at a crossing that is marked or not, In front of a driveway, on a sidewalk, or partially blocking a sidewalk, three feet from a wheelchair-accessible sidewalk ramp on the sidewalk in front of or adjacent to a curb that permits wheelchair access adjacent to a parking spot dedicated to the disabled, in the area indicated with crosshatched (diagonal lines) Unless you are running a zero-emission automobile, at a place dedicated for parking or fuelling zero-emission cars in a bridge or a tunnel, unless expressly noted by signs. within fifteen feet of a fire station driveway or fire hydrant. between the curb and a safety zone.

Parked twice.

except in circumstances of emergency, on the wrong side of the road, or a highway.

when a stop is asked by a law enforcement authority.

when it is specifically authorized to cease.

If you have to pull over on a highway, park your vehicle totally off the pavement and keep the doors locked until help arrives. On a highway, an automobile that is stopped, stalled, or held stationary for more than four hours may be removed.

Electric Cars

Parking locations on public highways for electric vehicle charging could be allotted by municipal authorities.

Traveling in Green

- By utilizing these tactics, you may optimize your fuel efficiency and contribute to cutting emissions:
- Accelerate and decelerate smoothly. Go at a consistent speed.
- Check filters, refill your oil, and inflate your tires regularly.
- Remove any additional weight from your automobile.
- When performing a law enforcement stop, law enforcement stops
- To communicate to the police that you have noticed them, flip on your right turn signal.
- Even if you are in the carpool/HOV lane, completely move to the right shoulder. When at all practical, stop in a well-lit spot.
- Switch off the radio.

Unless the police orders you to get out of your vehicle, remain inside.

After you stop your vehicle and before the cops reach you, pull down your window.

Before the police make contact with the driver or any other passenger, they should all place their hands in plain sight.

Law enforcement authorities will have to explain the cause of a traffic or pedestrian stop before interrogating someone about a criminal investigation or traffic infringement beginning on January 1, 2024. If an officer has a reasonable opinion that hiding the cause is essential to safeguard lives or property from an imminent risk, they are entitled to make an exception. The ticket that is issued or the law enforcement report that is prepared must explain the stop.

What You Can Do During an Enforcement Stop

You have the right to refuse to do anything an officer wants you to do.
 You do not, however, have the right to disrupt the officer's operations if you reject and they persist on going regardless of your objections. An officer might ask to search all or a piece of your automobile, for instance. Even if you have the right to refuse, there are scenarios in which the police may be lawfully entitled to search your automobile. If you oppose the police searching your automobile, you should be extremely vocal about it. However, if the police search your vehicle anyway, you have no right to fight back or obstruct them.

When a car is pulled over by the police, the driver is expected to present identity, documentation of insurance, and the registration of the vehicle.

Officers may perform a limited search for these documents if a driver refuses to furnish them. Additionally, a passenger's name or identification may be sought by an officer. Although passengers have the choice to deny this request, in certain cases they might still be required to give identification. Passengers should specifically say if they do not wish to share their identification. When an officer performs a traffic stop, passengers are required to assist with their actions and not get in the way of their demands for identification. An officer has the legal power to order the driver and every passenger to get out of the vehicle or stay inside it during a traffic stop. You have to heed any directions to get out of the automobile or stay inside.

Only federal law enforcement agents in California are permitted to ask about your immigration status.

It is prohibited for state and local law enforcement personnel in California to inquire drivers or passengers about their immigration status. You have the freedom to decline to answer queries about your immigration status from law enforcement in California.

The First Amendment typically protects motorists' and passengers' rights to record contacts with police personnel in public locations.

It should be clear immediately away if you are recording. During the enforcement stop, you have no right to disrupt the officer's legal responsibilities, and you shouldn't reach into concealed locations to grab your recording equipment until the officer gives you permission to. An officer cannot take your recording equipment, delete the recording, or destroy the device only because you are using it to record if it is not inhibiting the officer's ability to properly carry out their responsibilities. In theory, you also have the right to resist demands to unlock mobile phones or give passwords to them; yet, in specific cases, including when you are on parole, you might have to provide such requests. Finally, just because you filmed something publicly, doesn't imply a government employee may attempt retribution on you.

Even if you believe the police violated your rights, you shouldn't employ physical action or resistance against them.

You have the right to object to an officer's conduct that you believe violates your rights, but you shouldn't damage them with physical force. During a traffic stop, everyone has the right to feel safe. If there is physical resistance or violence in the situation, both your safety and the officer's safety may be at risk. It is prohibited for any government employee to take legal action against you for submitting a complaint against any law enforcement agency; everyone has the right to do so. The law enforcement body that employs the officer is the receiver of your complaint. Regarding your true or perceived race, sex, color, ethnicity, national origin, age, religion, gender identity or expression, sexual orientation, physical or mental impairment, health condition, or citizenship status, you have the right to be free from discrimination. The Constitutions of the United States and California, as well as state and federal statutes, also guarantee additional rights to you. The organization that employs the officer is expected to look into the concerns you submit.

Chapter 4: Understanding Vehicle Operation

Vehicle Controls and Gauges

1. Your hands contact the navigator's baton and the steering wheel. Touch its feel and pay heed to its delicate hints. The wheel turn commences the symphony, directing the car's route through the rhythmic flow of the road.

2. The accelerator and brake pedals are situated beneath your feet and regulate the driving rhythm. The brake pedal depresses quietly as the automobile comes to a gentle standstill, and the accelerator crescendos as it drives you onward.

3. The clutch takes center stage in the manual gearbox dance, masterfully choreographing the shift between gears. Press and release this vital element to exactly synchronize the motion of your automobile.

4. The shift lever, a writer crafting the tale of your voyage. Shift between gears and create the story of your acceleration and deceleration as you make your way across the next terrain.

5. One pause in the symphony is the parking brake. Press it to make the automobile motionless for a short time so you may step away and trust it to remain stable.

6. Headlights burst through the darkness to highlight the route ahead, while wipers dance over the glass to clear the way of pouring precipitation, producing a beautiful homage to your journeys.

7. A communicator in the symphony is the turn signal. Transmit your intentions to other drivers with a flick, coordinating the collective traffic dance.

8. Mirrors that reflect the harmony of your surroundings. To offer a symmetrical view of the road's evolving composition, tweak them to form a panoramic tableau.

9. An ensemble of gauges, that is the instrument cluster. Observe how the temperature, fuel, speed, and tachometers work together to give you an immediate performance and health score for your automobile.

10. The composers of the environment, climate controllers. Modify the temperature and vents to create a setting that improves your vacation and provides comfort as you pass through varied areas.

Every knob and gauge in this automotive symphony adds individually to the production of a safe, snug, and pleasant ride. Driving becomes a serene, absorbing experience when you become good at this symphony and steer the automobile along the intriguing courses of the open road.

Basic Vehicle Maintenance

Inspection of the Vehicle

The Need to Examine

The major motive for examining your automobile is safety both your own and other drivers.

An inspection-disclosed automobile fault can save you trouble down the line. It's conceivable that the defect may result in an accident that costs money and time, or worse, you may have a breakdown while driving.

Drivers must evaluate their autos as required by both federal and state standards. Your autos might potentially be examined by state and federal inspectors. The automobile will be put "out-of-service" until it is corrected if they think that it is harmful.

An automotive inspection may aid you in spotting faults that might result in an accident or malfunction. Before utilizing a vehicle, routine checkups should be undertaken. Read the report from the most recent automobile inspection. Verify whether the maintenance professionals have given the automobile the all-clear to be serviced. Any flaws in the report that influence safety must be repaired by the motor carrier, who must also testify on the report that such repairs were necessary or were accomplished. Keep in mind that it is your responsibility not the mechanic's to drive the automobile safely when you get behind the wheel. Sign the preceding driver's report if the problems have been repaired.

To travel securely, you ought to:

- Check gauges for indicators of abnormalities.
- Check for difficulties with your senses (see, hear, smell, and feel).
- When you stop, take a look at these vital things: wheels, rims, and tires.
- reflectors and lights.
- electrical and braking connections were added to the trailer
- equipment for joining trailers.
- freight safety measures.

After the journey, day, or duty tour, you need to complete an after-trip inspection on every vehicle you drive. It might entail completing a vehicle condition report and documenting any concerns you uncover. A motor carrier may decide when the vehicle needs repairs with the assistance of the inspection report.

Points to Consider

Tire Issues

- Insufficient or excessive air pressure.
- Unhealthy wear. Every important groove on the front tires needs to have at least 4/32 inches of tread depth. On other tires, 2/32 inch is necessary. There should be no fabric showing through the sidewall or tread.
- wounds or other injuries.
- Separate your tread.
- two tires that make contact with one another or other components of the automobile.

- different dimensions tires with bias ply and radial tread combination cracked or damaged valve stems.
- tire regrooved, recapped, or retreaded on a bus's front wheels. These are not permitted.

Issues with the Wheel and Rim

- damaged wheel components.
- Wheel nuts may be loose if there is corrosion around them; ensure sure they are secure. After replacing a tire, take a minute to stop and double-check that the nuts are tight.
- Danger develops when studs, lugs, clamps, or spacers are missing.
- It is dangerous to utilize lock rings that are misshapen, misaligned, or damaged.
- Welding repairs on wheels or rims hinder safety.

defective brake shoes or drums that crack.

- Shoes or pads coated in brake fluid, oil, or grease.
- Shoes that are broken, missing, or dangerously thin.
- Bugs in the Steering System
- missing cotter keys, bolts, nuts, or other components.
- parts including tie rods, the steering gearbox, and the steering column that is deformed, loose, or broken.
- Verify the fluid level, hoses, pumps, and leaks if the vehicle has power steering.
- It may be difficult to steer if there is more than 10 degrees of steering wheel play, or roughly 2 inches of movement at the rim of

a 20-inch steering wheel.

Faults in the Suspension System

- The axles are retained in place and the vehicle and its load are supported by the suspension system. As a consequence, damaged suspension components may be highly dangerous.

Seek out:
- An axle can depart from its optimal position owing to spring hangers.
- Spring hangers that are damaged or fractured.
- any leaf spring with damaged or missing leaves. The automobile will be deemed "out-of-service" if one-fourth or more are gone, although any defect may be detrimental.

A multi-leaf spring with damaged leaves or leaves that have shifted and could collide with a tire or other component.

Shock absorbers that leak.

- Axle positioning components that are damaged, missing, or cracked include torque rods or arms, u-bolts, spring hangers, and other components.
- air suspension systems with leaks or other difficulties. any missing, broken, loose, or damaged frame components.

Fixes for Exhaust Systems
- Poison fumes may infiltrate the sleeping bunk or cab owing to a defective exhaust system. Seek out:
- vertical stacks, mufflers, tailpipes, and exhaust pipes that are loose, broken, or missing.
- Bolts, nuts, clamps, and mounting brackets that are loose, damaged, or missing.

- Tires, fuel system components, and other moving sections of the automobile could rub against exhaust system components.

components of the exhaust system that leak.

Emergency Provisions

- An emergency kit is a necessity for automobiles. Seek out:
- Extinguisher(s) for fire.
- extra electrical fuses (if not already installed with circuit breakers).
- Devices for notifying parked automobiles (e.g., six fuses, three liquid-burning flares, or three red reflective warning triangles).

Test for CDL Vehicle Inspection

- You will need to pass a vehicle inspection test to earn a CDL. Your ability to judge whether your automobile is safe to drive will be tested. You will be needed of you to check your automobile. You must identify the object you are inspecting, point to it or touch it, and give the examiner an explanation of why. The seven-step assessment technique that follows ought to be useful.
- Truckloads of goods. Before every travel, you have to make sure the truck is not overloaded and the cargo is properly tied. Inspect the cargo for necessary documentation and placarding if it comprises Hazardous items.

A Seven-Step Inspection Process

Inspection Technique. Every time you examine an automobile, apply the same approach to guarantee you understand every step and limit the potential of forgetting anything.

Going up to the Car. Take notice of the general condition. Check for any damage or sideways movement in the automobile. Check for leaks in the fuel, coolant, fresh oil, or grease beneath the vehicle. Look around the automobile for anything that can interfere with its ability to drive, such as people, other cars, things, low-hanging wires, trees, etc.

➢ Guide to Vehicle Inspection

Step 1: Overview of the Vehicle

Examine the report from the most recent car inspection. It might be essential for drivers to fill up a daily report on vehicle inspections. Any flaws in the report that influence safety must be repaired by the motor carrier, who must also testify on the report that such repairs were necessary or were accomplished. If any flaws were detected and considered repairable, or if no repairs are necessary, you will merely be asked to sign the report.

Step 2: Examine the engine compartment, Make ensure the wheels are chocked or that the parking brakes are engaged. To keep goods from dropping and shattering, you may need to tilt the cab, raise the hood, or open the engine compartment door. Verify the following:

- level of engine oil.
- Condition of the hoses and the radiator's coolant level.
- The condition of the hose (if given) and the quantity of power steering fluid.
- fluid level of the windshield washer.

Tie-downs, connections, and the fluid level of the battery (which may be elsewhere).

Automatic leveling of the transmission fluid (may require the engine to run).

Examine belts (air compressor, water pump, alternator) for excessive wear and tightness. Determine the optimal amount of "give" for each belt and check them all.

Check the engine compartment for leaks in the hydraulic, battery, power steering, coolant, and oil.

Insulation for electrical wire to avoid wear and fractures.

The hood, cab, or engine compartment door should be lowered and fastened.

Step 3: Turn on the engine and examine the cabin inside

- Enter and turn on the engine
- Verify that the parking brake is engaged.
- Select Neutral on the gearbox (or "Park" if it's automatic).
- Start the engine and keep an ear open for unusual noises.
- Verify the anti-lock braking system (ABS) indicator lights if your car has them. The dash light ought to illuminate before switching off. If it stays on, there is an issue with the ABS. For trailers only: the ABS is malfunctioning if the yellow light on the left rear of the trailer stays on.

Examine the Gauges

oil pressure. The engine should start and the pressure should return to normal air force. In three minutes, pressure should build from 50 to 90 pounds per square inch (psi). Determine the air pressure required for your automobile and build it to the governor cut-out pressure, which is frequently between 120 and 140 psi.

- A voltmeter or an ammeter. Must fall within the predicted range.
- the temperature of the coolant. should start to ascend gradually to the average operating range.

- temperature of engine oil. should start to ascend gradually to the average operating range.
- Buzzers and warning lights. The ABS, coolant, oil, and charging circuit warning lights need to be switched off promptly.

Examine the controls' condition

Examine each of the following for damage, sticking, looseness, or wrong setting:
- steering mechanism.
- clutch.
- gas pedal, or accelerator.
- brake controls
- Brake with the foot.
- If the automobile has a trailer brake.

The parking brake
- Retarder controls if equipped to the automobile.
- controls for the transmission.
- differential lock between the axles (if the automobile has one).
- Horn(s).
- windshield washer and wiper.

Plugs in
- Headlights.
- Dimmer toggle.
- Make a turn signal.
- 4-way flashers for emergencies.
- Marker switch(es), parking, clearance, and identification.
- Check the windshield and mirrors.
- Examine the windshield and mirrors for any cracks, dust, unapproved stickers, or other material that may impair your vision. As required, clean up and make modifications.

Examine the emergency supplies
- Look for safety gear:
- additional electrical fuses, if the automobile doesn't have circuit breakers.
- Six fuses, three red reflecting triangles, or three liquid-burning flares.
- fire extinguisher that is suitably rated and charged.

Look for optional components, like
- Chains (when chilly weather necessitates them).
- equipment for changing tires.

- A list of phone numbers for emergencies.
- package for reporting accidents.

Examine the seat belt

- Verify that the safety belt is not damaged or frayed, is secured tightly, and adjusts, and locks appropriately.

Step 4: Check the lights and switch off the engine

- Turn off the engine, ensure sure the parking brake is engaged, and then remove the key. After turning on the 4-way emergency flashers and low-beam headlights, leave the automobile.

Step 5: Conduct an Inspection Walkthrough

- Verify that the low beams are on and both of the 4-way flashers are working by approaching the front of the car:
- Make certain the high beams are operating by pulling the dimmer button.
- Switch off the 4-way emergency flashers and the headlights.
- Activate the side marker, parking, clearing, and identifying lights.
- Initiate the walk-around inspection and activate the right turn signal.

Overall

- Take a peek around and check the automobile.
- As you proceed, wipe clean all of the lights, reflectors, and glass.

Front side left

- The driver's door glass needs to be pristine.
- Locks and latches on doors should work appropriately.

Front left wheel

- Wheel and rim condition: no clamps, lugs, missing, bent, or broken spacer studs, nor any signs of misalignment.

Tire condition

- correctly inflated, tread wear, no noticeable cuts or bulges, and intact valve stem and cap.
- To verify whether rust-streaked lug nuts are loose, use a wrench.
- Alright hub oil level and no leaks.
- Front Suspension on the Left
- condition of u-bolts, shackles, spring hangers, and springs.
- Shock absorber state.
- Front left brake
- condition of the brake disk or drum.
- status of the hose systems.

condition of the front axle.

- condition of the steering mechanism.

- No missing, twisted, worn-out, broken, or loose components.
- To check for looseness, one must grab the steering mechanism.
- State of the Windscreen
- Examine for damage and clean if required.
- Verify the right spring tension on the wiper arms on the windshield.
- Examine the wiper blades for damage, rubber that is "stiff," and tightness.
- Reflectors and Lights
- The lights for parking, clearing, and identification are in excellent shape, and functioning, and the right color amber in front.
- The front-facing amber reflectors are sharp and have the perfect tone.
- The front turn signal light on the right is working, immaculate, and the proper color—amber or white for signals pointing forward.

Side to the right

- Verify every item on the right front is finished for the left front.
- If the design is cab-over-engine, both primary and secondary safety cab locks are engaged.

Correct fuel tank or tanks

- Firmly fastened, undamaged, and leak-free.
- The Crossover line for gasoline is safe.
- Fuel is present in adequate tank(s).
- The cap(s) is on and locked.

State of the Visible Parts

- The engine's back is not leaking.
- There is no leakage in the transmission.
- The exhaust system is safe, leak-free, and maintained away from fuel, electrical, and airlines.
- There are no fractures or bends in the cross members or frame.
- Electrical and airlines are shielded from rubbing, snagging, and wearing.
- If equipped, the spare tire carrier or rack is intact.
- A spare wheel or tire is securely secured in the rack.
- The spare wheel and tire are adequate (correct size, proper pressure).

Securing Cargo (Trucks)

- The cargo is securely secured, roped, braced, blocked, etc.
- The header board (if required) is secure and acceptable.
- Stakes and sideboards are in excellent shape, suitably robust, and positioned appropriately (if fitted).
- Make sure the canvas or tarp if necessary is properly attached to minimize tearing, flapping, or blocking mirrors.

- If the vehicle is bigger than typical, the driver has the relevant permits and all signs (lamps, reflectors, and flags) are securely and properly mounted.
- The cargo compartment doors on the curbside are in perfect order, locked or latched solidly, and have the essential security seals fitted.

Right Back

- Wheel and rim condition: no spacers, studs, clamps, or lugs missing, bent, or damaged.
- In excellent shape with no severe cuts, bulges, or tread wear, the tires not rubbing against one another, and nothing stuck between them. The valve stems and covers are also in place.
- Tires are of the same kind they're not mixed radial and bias sorts, for instance.
- The tires are matched properly (same size).
- Seals and wheel bearings don't leak.

Hanging

- State of the U-bolts, shackles, spring hangers, and springs.
- Secure axle(s).
- The motorized axle or axles do not have gear oil leaks.
- State of bushings and torque rod arms.
- The condition of one or more shock absorbers.
- Verify the lift mechanism's condition if the axle is retractable. If utilizing air power, search for any leaks.
- status of the air ride's components.

Stops

- Brake adjustment.
- status of the brake discs or drums.
- Condition of the hoses: check for any rubbing-related damage.

Reflectors and Lights

- The side marker lights are functioning, immaculate, and the proper color—amber on the others, and red at the rear.
- Cleanliness and suitable color (red at the back, amber elsewhere) define side marker reflectors.
- The rear clearance and identification lights (which are red in the back) are clear, effective, and have the proper tone.
- Reflectors are immaculate and the proper color (red at the rear).
- The taillights are functioning, immaculate, and the proper color—red on the rear.
- The right rear turn signals are on and the proper color is visible at the back (amber, yellow, or red).

- The license plate or plates are there, nice, and secure.

There are splash guards; they're undamaged, firmly linked, not dragging on the ground, and they don't scrape against the tires.

During the automobile inspection test, why did you put the starting switch key in your pocket?

You may have to answer these on your test. Reread if you are unable to react to every one of them.

Handling Emergencies and Breakdowns

1. Firmly press the brake pedal.
2. As soon as the car begins to skid, release the brake swiftly. Next, apply pressure once more.
3. Continue to aggressively pump the brakes until the car stops.
4. Don't apply a strong brake and hold.

An automobile is approaching you in your lane.

1. If you have time, inform the other driver by blasting your horn and flashing your lights.
2. Apply the brakes rapidly without locking up and losing control.
3. Veer off the road into the right shoulder or ditch if the other car continues to approach and a collision is probable. Keep out of the left lane when driving.

Driving a Car While Intoxicated

1. You may help if the automobile in front of you continues attempting to pass by slowing down and driving as safely to the right as you can.
2. Pick up the speed to enable the other driver to cover the space behind you if he is unable to complete the pass and needs to drop back.
3. Move fast onto the right shoulder to enable the passing car into your lane if it is safe to do so and a collision is nearly likely.

Back-end collisions

1. Be prepared to compress the brakes to prevent being driven into the car in front of you.
2. Place your arms between the headrest and the driving wheel.
3. Firmly force your head back against the headrest.

Side-impact Accidents

1. Hold onto the steering wheel tightly. By behaving accordingly, you may escape being hurled against the car's side.
2. Prepare to steer fast so that you may try to regain control of the car in the case of a spin.

Directly Collisions

1. If you have your shoulder strap and seat belt on, use your hands and arms to cover your face.
2. To avoid contacting the windshield or steering wheel, throw yourself across the seat if you are not wearing your shoulder strap.

Getting Over a Skid

1. Avoid applying the brakes.
2. Release the accelerator pedal.
3. Only spin the front wheel far enough to prevent them from driving in a straight path. Turn the front wheels to the right if your car's rear is sliding to the right. To ski to the left, turn left.
4. Take caution not to steer too much. It might begin to slip oppositely. Turn your wheels in the skid's direction once more. When the car is back under control, you can feel it. Next, align the wheels.

Leaping from the sidewalk

1. Use simply your brakes to slow down.
2. Steer back onto the road easily if there isn't a drop-off from the pavement.
3. Should the shoulder dip severely below the pavement:
4.Go very gently at first
5.After making sure there is no approaching traffic, suddenly shift your wheels back onto the   pavement.

Blowout in tires.

1. Maintain a firm hold on the steering wheel and drive in the same lane. A considerable drag to the left or right could occur.
2. Allow the car to decelerate. Wait until you've slowed down to a safe speed before activating the brakes.
3. Next, apply a gentle brake and completely leave the car in a specified safe zone.
Sticks for Gas Pedals
1. Select neutral for the gear shift.

126　　　　

2. Attempt to use your foot to release the pedal. If you are unable to release it, ask your

Brakes Not Working

1. Quickly push the pedal; after that
2. Change into a smaller gear.
3. Search for a route out. Make use of your lights and horns to inform other cars.
4. While retaining the brake release lever in the release position, gently apply the parking brakes.

Use your hand to steer by putting it on top of the steering wheel.
Avoid applying the parking brake suddenly. The automobile may lose control as a result of this.
Loss of the Wheel is the same procedure as a blown tire.

Engine Overheating

Keep the radiator cap closed.
Flames
1. Drive away from other traffic and come to a standstill.
2. Cut all electrical switches and the engine.
3. Exit the automobiles and guide all passengers elsewhere. The automobile could be packed with poisonous gasses.
4. If the fire is minor, smother it with clothing, earth, mud, or a chemical fire extinguisher. Never throw water on an electrical, oil, or fuel fire.
5. You may not be able to put out a huge gasoline or oil fire. Don't try; ask for support instead.

Taking a Diving Board into Water

1. To breathe, go within the air pocket.
2. It is easier to open a door or window after the car settles and the pressure inside and outside is equal.
3. Keep in mind that you might have a few minutes to spare. It may be feasible to escape away if you don't panic.

Defunct Battery

Verify that the two automobiles are not in touch.
1. Jumping off a dead battery raises the danger of significant harm.
2. Remove the vent covers on each battery. Cover the exposed vent wells with a cloth.
3. Switch off the radio, heating, and lights.

4. Join the dead battery's positive post to the surviving battery's positive post.

5. Attach the live battery's negative post to the dead battery's negative post, the engine block, or the frame.

Get the jump car started. Give it a few minutes to run. Next, oppositely remove the cables and reattach the vent covers. The cloth covering the vent wells should be thrown away.

Dissections

Place flares on the side of the road at least 100 feet behind your car at night. To improve your safety, set flares close to, 100 feet ahead of, and along the side of the road. If you are traveling alone at night, remain in your car for safety, and be suspicious of the help given.

When it's sunlight, raise the hood and tie a white cloth to the left door handle or radio antenna to signify that your car has broken down. Generally speaking, it is advisable to stay in your car and wait outside in a safe spot.

Mishaps

1. Come to a sudden halt and introduce yourself.

2. Assist those who are harmed. When in doubt, presume that an ambulance is necessary.

3. Information interchange. If questioned, you must supply your name, address, and vehicle's

license number. Inform your insurance provider, and if you feel worried, visit a physician.

Keep the following in mind if you are not trained in first aid

1. Request help.

2. Make an attempt to aid the injured in the order that their needs are outlined. Maintain their warmth.

3. Cover the wound with a clean cloth to stop the bleeding.

4. If you are able, administer first aid if the patient's breathing has ceased.

5. Unless there is an urgent risk to the injured person's life, do not move them. More injuries could come from moving.

6. Request that a person who is limping sit or rest on his back. Turn the patient onto his side if there is bleeding from the jaw or lower area of the face. Give no fluids at all.

7. Unless there is no other way to seek help, you should not try to carry an injured person to the hospital. In situations of serious injuries, inappropriate movement could be hazardous.

Environmental Considerations and Fuel Efficiency Tips

Verify the pressure in your tires.

- Although they may not seem connected, your car requires more fuel to move when the pressure on your tires is lower.
- Make sure your tires are at the right pressure once every two weeks by inspecting them; the owner's manual or glovebox normally contains information on this.
- Verify that the gear you are in is the lowest speed or highest gear.
- Driving in the highest gear at the slowest feasible speed is the ideal strategy to achieve the best mpg.
- The car will need to work harder and consume more fuel the faster you travel. being early and having to refill is considerably worse than being on time and wasting more gas!

Use the air conditioner less frequently

- The air conditioner is another fuel-sucker that is not easily noticeable. Even though having a car with temperature control in December might seem wonderful, the truth is that it's undoubtedly pricey, so assess whether it's truly worth it.

Take off the roof rack

- This is another obvious concept: when you travel at a high speed, drag is enhanced by the weight of the stuff on top of your car.
- As a consequence, the car will drag back, demanding more work to maintain motion and speed and ultimately costing you more in fuel.
- Therefore, if you are not going to need the skis, bikes, or roof rack for that trip, make sure to remove them.

Lessen the burden

- As previously noted, your car will have to work harder to transfer greater goods, especially when traveling uphill.
- Therefore, removing unnecessary weight takes more than merely taking off the roof rack. More gasoline will be required to power the vehicle to counteract the added weight.

- Make sure everything that isn't essential for your travel has been removed ahead to preserve gas. Look in the boot of your car for any overlooked goods that could be squandering more fuel.
- Keep in mind that an additional 50 kg will result in a 2% increase in fuel use on average, so those extras may soon stack up!

Get a car that consumes less fuel.
- Buying a new, energy-efficient car should be on your list of things to do if you want to lower your fuel bills over time.
- You are more likely to be able to buy a vehicle that gets better gas mileage as manufacturers are increasingly considering energy economy and environmental friendliness when building new models.
- A contemporary car will also require less maintenance and presumably have more sophisticated technology, which will save you even more petroleum.

Make a route plan
- If you are aware of your destination in advance, invest some time to design the most effective path.
- This isn't always the shortest option; if you know that your town will be packed with traffic during rush hour, plan beforehand and take the back roads instead of the established path. It may end up being quicker than being trapped in traffic.
- Similar to how an engine operates more effectively when it's warm, plan brief outings and errands simultaneously to allow you to make one longer journey rather than numerous little ones.
- This may appear paradoxical, but it will save fuel as the engine won't have to work as hard to continuously warm up and cool down.

Keep up the pace
- Similar to this, driving with momentum will result in greater fuel efficiency.
- Continuously accelerating and decelerating will enhance the fuel demand for the car's functioning, resulting in considerably greater fuel consumption.
- You can keep going forward by being prepared and examining the way ahead of you, which will inform you of oncoming impediments.

Verify the condition of your tires
- Maintaining tire pressure and ensuring sure your tires are in great condition with plenty of treads and no balding or nicks are identical to this.

- They will be able to grip and move on the road more efficiently as a consequence, which will save you money and, most importantly, assure safety!

Switch it off
- The engine is still burning fuel whether you are stalled in traffic, waiting to turn off a crossroads, or picking up a passenger. You are not going ahead.
- If you will be waiting more than ten seconds, switch off the engine and start it as soon as you know you are driving to preserve fuel.
- Because you're not leaving the car running aimlessly, this is not only a simple approach to decreasing fuel usage, but it also helps limit pollution!

Chapter 5: Special Driving Situations

Driving in Inclement Weather

It's typical to have severe weather and risky driving conditions. Practicing safe driving habits in common winter weather scenarios, like rain, wind, snow, ice, sleet, and fog, is more vital than ever. Practicing safety is even more vital during extreme weather occurrences like electrical storms, hurricanes, tornadoes, and deluges of rain or snow. If there is an extreme weather system going through your area, it is advisable to defer a trip and stay home instead of traveling.

Make early arrangements. It generally takes longer and is more uncomfortable to drive in bad weather. If you are running late because you did not give enough time to get to your place, this will merely make you more agitated and may possibly affect your driving. Check the weather before you travel as well. If you can avoid the worst of a weather system by traveling an alternate route, do so. You may also want to consider about postponing your trip when the weather clears up. If you choose not to postpone, make sure you carry a map with you to assist you find your route if visibility is poor and to prevent you from getting lost.

Travel at a Slow Speed. This goes hand in hand with the previous rule; in severe weather, drive more slowly than usual. As a consequence, there are fewer skids and accidents.

Make Space Up Front. When driving in precipitation such as rain, sleet, or snow, many experts suggest expanding the "cushion" between your car and the one in front of you by two. In these instances, you have to allow yourself more space because the brake reaction time is slower.

Verify that the equipment you have is functioning. In the winter, get your brakes and tires checked more regularly. Verify that your headlights are clean and that your windshield wipers are in excellent operational order. Visibility may be substantially diminished by filthy headlights, especially in bad weather. Before you travel, remove any ice or frost from your windshield and mirrors, and use wipers and wiper fluid to keep them clean while you're driving. Make sure you stop in a safe spot if you need to scrape ice or snow off of your car.

In fog, use your low beams. Whether you are driving in fog during the day or at night, put on your headlights and make sure you use your low beams instead of your high beams. Your low beam headlights improve in both your visibility and that of other motorists. In addition, you should drive cautiously and preserve a wide following distance in fog as you may not see a traffic light or another motorist until it is practically upon you. When there is fog, remain close to the right side of the road to avoid crossing the center line and into oncoming traffic.

Turn on the radio. While driving, tone down the noise and listen in to a radio station that gives information on road conditions. The station might let you know about traffic limitations or propose alternate routes. You must drive especially carefully in stormy weather, so set the music down to prevent distracting yourself.

Travel at a Slow Speed. This goes hand in hand with the previous rule; in severe weather, drive more slowly than usual. As a consequence, there are fewer skids and accidents.

Fasten your seat belt! Make sure you constantly buckle up, as well as your passengers. It can save lives and is mandatory by law in most places, especially when driving in adverse weather.

Should You Need to, Stop. If you're even marginally fatigued, stop (safely, entirely off the road) and give your eyes a rest. It's better to "waste" a little time by pulling over than to risk getting into an accident, so don't be terrified of it. Additionally, it could be a good idea to identify a safe area to pull off the road and try to wait out a sudden unfavorable weather trend. Make sure you are not stopping into a deep puddle or snow bank if the severe weather includes heavy snow or a lot of rain.

Navigating Freeways and Highways

Your doorway to the highway sonata is the entry ramp. As you easily move into the flow, you'll feel the acceleration a taste of the pace that's to come.

The harmony in motion is specified by the lanes, which are akin to musical staves on sheet music. Drive with precision, picking the proper lane for your pace, and easing into and out of traffic as the highway regulates the flow.

 merging points: areas where automobiles play together like a band. Find your space in the traffic symphony, announce your intentions, and coordinate your actions.

transcending, a growing crescendo. Determine the pace of incoming traffic, move smoothly, and fade into the background like a fleeting note in a song.

Conversations, the musical twists on your journey. As you make your way through the complicated passages and elegantly transition from one action to the next, follow the suggestions.

The magnificent breaks and wayside views that are part of the route composition. Observe the moving environment, which incorporates both rural and metropolis skylines, each of which extends a different movement within the symphony.

ramps for departure, a falling movement when you are about to go. Give notice of your purpose, ease off the highway ramp, and turn into local streets.

Rest breaks are quiet pauses along the road. Before going on to the next movement, take a time to recharge and allow the symphony to breathe.

Traffic flow, a coordinated group. Be conscious of other passengers' behavior and maintain a group cadence to assure a tranquil and enjoyable ride.

The glorious culmination of the highway symphony is your arrival. Drive the remaining few kilometers with precision, finishing your vehicle song elegantly when you reach your destination.

You are the conductor and composer while driving on freeways and highways, organizing your car across the various lanes, crossroads, and gorgeous portions. Every movement of the highway symphony becomes a chapter in the enthralling drama of your voyage, giving it a memorable and musical experience while you drive.

Sharing the Road with Pedestrians and Cyclists

Pedestrians

Pedestrians have the right-of-way in a variety of scenarios. These include when a pedestrian is at a pelican crossing, is waiting to cross at a zebra crossing, or is already across the road while the amber light is flashing.

In these conditions, automobiles and motorcycles should always yield to pedestrians and, of course, stop at a pair of red pedestrian lights. Paths are only designed for use by pedestrians. Driving totally or partly onto a sidewalk is illegal unless you need to cross it to enter a structure. Do this only when it's secure. Respecting vulnerable road users demands attentiveness. Pedestrians may be unpredictable and may not always be visible when they attempt to cross the street, such as when they emerge from between two parked automobiles or get off the bus. You allow yourself more time to react to unanticipated risks by slowing down in locations where there are many of people, including towns and cities. The movements of youngsters are extremely unpredictable. When driving in situations where children might be present, such as in parks and schools, in parking lots, and in residential estates, pay special attention and slow down. Smaller children cannot be seen in your rearview mirror or via the back window while you are reversing; if you are at all doubtful, get out and check behind you. Be patient and give them time to cross the road safely as they are more vulnerable than other drivers, particularly the elderly and those with disabilities.

Motorcyclists and cyclists

Drivers are expected to share the road with motorcyclists and cyclists without endangering them, according to the Rules of the Road guideline. Checking your mirrors and blind spots is one of the greatest ways to be more alert, particularly in the following situations: changing lanes or reversing at intersections; stopping and turning, especially to the left; opening your door to get out of your car; and when a cycle lane ends and joins with the road.

Driving over a bicycle requires you to maintain a safe passing distance, which is 1.5 meters when driving over 50 mph and at least 1 meter while traveling under that speed. When passing groups of bicycles or bikers pedaling two abreast, employ extreme care. If you wish to turn left at a junction, avoid passing a bicycle. Similarly, be aware of bicyclists heading your way on the opposite side of the road when you're crossing it to make a right. Bicyclists sometimes face the danger of "dooring," which happens when they hit with an open automobile door. When you depart your car, make it a routine to employ "the Dutch Reach." This safety practice, which is well entrenched in Dutch driving culture, requires the driver to glance in their mirror and over their shoulder before exiting the car by opening the door with their far hand—or, in Ireland, their left hand. Although it's a simple procedure, it saves lives. Remember that weather has a bigger influence on motorcyclists and cyclists than on vehicles. They are more likely to be blown off course in heavy gusts, and they are more prone to lose control of the car on wet or icy roads. They may have to adjust their path to avoid potholes on the side of the road if the road is badly maintained.

Cycle lanes

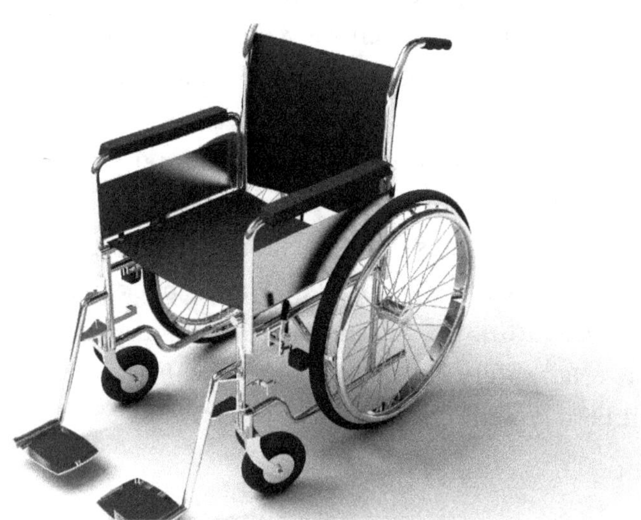

Cycle lanes are designed for persons using motorized wheelchairs or bicycles, and their goal is to protect these road users from approaching vehicles. There are two sort of bike lanes, and each has specific regulations: A cycle track is needed by the Rules of the Road and is described as a bike lane that is a continuous white line isolated from the rest of the road. Any other user of the road, including motorcycle riders, should not cross it unless they need to get to or from a business or side road. Parking on a designated bike route is forbidden because it puts cyclists at danger. A broken white line represents non-mandatory bicycle tracks, which are denoted by other bike lanes. When it's safe to do so and there are no cyclists using them already, automobiles are permitted to momentarily cross the broken white line. Drivers of goods trucks are permitted to park on this form of cycle track for a limited length of time, no more than 30 minutes, while loading or unloading their vehicle if there is no alternative parking available. Any blockage of a bike lane puts bikers at danger, hence as a vehicle, you have a duty to drive carefully and avoid areas assigned for riding.

Driving at Night and in Low Visibility

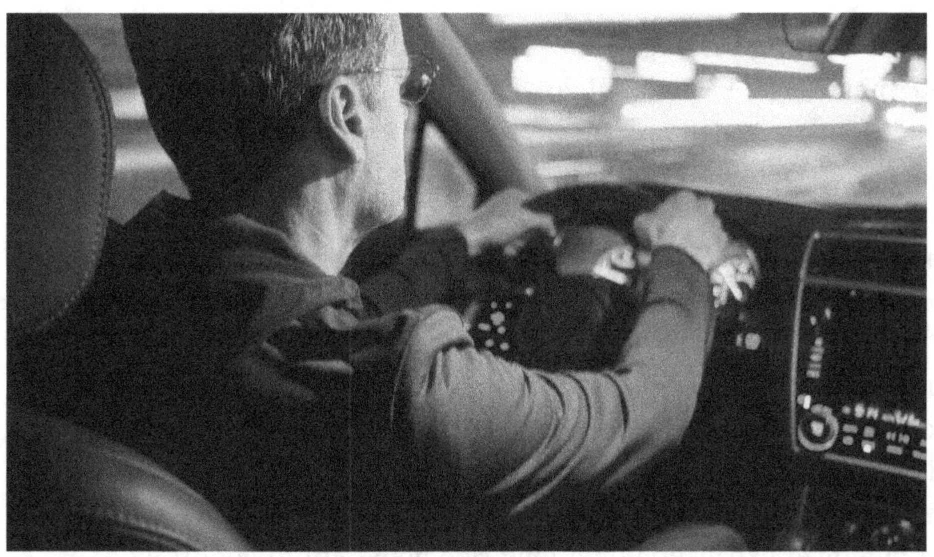

All drivers in California are obliged by law to use headlights for 30 minutes after nightfall and 30 minutes prior to dawn. Anytime you are unable to see more than 1,000 feet in front of your automobile, you must also switch on your headlights.

One of the issues when driving at night is reduced visibility or vision impairments.
At night, a driver's ability to discern depth, identify colors, and utilize their peripheral vision is severely impaired
1.Impaired eyesight may aggravate night vision and make it more difficult to view things correctly The high beams or headlights of other automobiles could cause eye discomfort In the dark, things look different and lose part of their sharpness.

2. Fatigue Issues Because they are typically drowsy at night, drivers are less vigilant, unable to focus, and slower to react to traffic threats, The chance of an accident increases when drivers react slowly to dangers because they are less likely to do so precisely and fast.

3. Impaired Motorists Some nocturnal drivers may drive carelessly after drinking because they have had one or more drinks Because they are inattentive, lack focus, react badly to traffic conditions, tailgate regularly, make poor judgments, and occasionally even stray into your lane, these drivers increase the probability of accidents on the roads at night. Therefore, employ care and avoid following or changing lanes suddenly, tailgating, or showing any other symptoms of driving while inebriated.

4. **Recommendations for safe evening driving**:
- Use headlights 30 minutes after nightfall and 30 minutes before dawn in compliance with California regulations. In any case where your eyesight is limited, including fog, rain, snow, twilight, snow, rain, and fog, you should also employ your headlights.
- Maintain the cleanliness of your windows, both inside and out. To decrease glare, it is especially vital to preserve the interior of your windows and windshield clean.
- Examine and ensure that every light in your automobile is behaving as it should.
- If you're weary, don't drive. When you're feeling too weary to drive, try to find a secure area to pull over and take a sleep.

Driving at night may be extremely tiring as it needs a significant lot of focus and concentration. In order to minimize exhaustion on a long ride home, try to get off the highway at regular intervals or stop at rest sites. You should also ensure that you are vigilant before starting driving.

Even if you are under the legal drinking limit, never drink and drive. Drinking may decrease your awareness and drowsiness, as well as slow down your reaction time in driving circumstances.

Be careful when driving after drinking and avoid them. Drunk drivers typically tailgate, drift into and out of lanes, and display other symptoms of impairment. Increase the spacing between your automobile and the one in front of you.
- Never overload your headlights by moving so swiftly that you are unable to stop within the beam's length.
- Use your high lights when driving on a freeway, a rural road, or a poorly lighted region. Do not use your high lights in fog, continuous incoming traffic, when there is a vehicle 500 feet away, or while you are following a car 300 feet distant.

- Never purposely switch on your bright lights to pass another automobile; you can both be dazzled and get into an accident.
- Don't try to get even with someone who is nasty with their headlights.
- Avert glancing directly into oncoming traffic's headlights.
- Keeping an eye on the car approaching from the corner of your eye, glance to the right edge of your lane.

Chapter 6: Driving Under the Influence and Other Offenses

Understanding DUI Laws and Consequences

Driving after drinking is a dangerous and reckless practice that has serious effects. Regretfully, a lot of folks don't know the serious legal and psychological ramifications of a DUI, In truth, a DUI may lead to significant legal repercussions including fines, license revocation, and even jail time. A DUI conviction may have long-term financial and psychological implications that will certainly haunt you for years to come. In order to prepare oneself for these allegations, it's necessary to know the complete breadth of DUI punishments.

Legal Repercussions for a DUI

Driving under the influence (DUI) is a severe criminal crime in California that carries significant sanctions. The following legal ramifications may occur in California if you are arrested for DUI:

License Suspension: In California, if you are arrested for driving under the influence, your license will generally be suspended for six months. The term of suspension is prolonged if this is your second or subsequent DUI.

Jail Time: The duration of your prison term will depend on the facts of your DUI conviction. In California, you may go to jail for up to six months if this is your first DUI offense. However, the duration of your jail term may grow substantially if your blood alcohol concentration (BAC) was greater than 0.15% or if driving under the influence resulted in damage or death.

Penalties and Court Expenses: In California, a DUI conviction involves severe fines and court expenditures. For a first-time DUI infraction, the minimum sentence is $390, but depending on the circumstances of the behavior, it may be as high as $1,000 or more.

Ignition Interlock Device: Installing an ignition interlock device (IID) in your automobile may be essential if you are found guilty of driving under the influence in California. In order to start your vehicle, you must blow into this device, which will not start your car if it detects alcohol on your breath.

DUI Education and Treatment Programs: People convicted guilty of a DUI in California are forced to undergo a DUI education and treatment program. The number of DUI offenses and other criteria will determine the program's length and degree of severity.

Criminal History In addition to having a severe impact on future career opportunities and housing applications, a DUI conviction in California will also result in a criminal record.

DUI's Financial Repercussions. A DUI conviction may result in substantial financial ramifications in addition to legal fines. Financial problems may be considerably worsened by penalties, court expenditures, higher insurance rates, and DUI education and treatment programs. A DUI conviction may also limit your professional growth and employment retention, losing you money and prospects down the line.

The Personal Repercussions of a DUI

A DUI conviction may result in long-term negative impacts on a person's reputation, mental distress, and interpersonal ties. The ramifications of a DUI may impact family members and loved ones, and the cultural stigma linked to a DUI may bring embarrassment and shame. By obtaining the services of a qualified criminal defense lawyer, you may decrease the repercussions of your DUI on your life and secure your future possibilities.

How Can a DUI Attorney Assist?

- It is vital that you receive legal assistance from an experienced DUI attorney if you are facing DUI charges.
- A DUI attorney may aid in a variety of ways, such as: defending your legal rights and making certain a fair trial examining the evidence against you to uncover flaws in the case established by the prosecution

establishing a powerful defense strategy that is customized to the particulars of your case negotiating a reduction of charges or penalties with prosecutors defending you in court and presenting an argument for you supplying guidance and help throughout the legal process

mitigating the financial, legal, and psychological impact from a DUI conviction

Distracted Driving Awareness

One of the road safety dangers that is developing the fastest at the present is distracted driving. Not only do inattentive drivers threaten their personal safety, but they also harm other road users. The purpose of the national campaign against distracted driving is to modify driver behavior via education, public awareness campaigns, law enforcement, and legislation.

Distracted driving has been prevalent on American roadways for the past ten years, placing not only the drivers themselves but also their passengers, bystanders, and other road users, including bicyclists, in hazard.

Although there are numerous distractions and changes in life, we only need to focus on driving safely when we are behind the wheel. You are distracted when you take your eyes off the road. This encompasses conversing, texting, using your phone, navigating, adjusting the radio, putting on cosmetics, eating, and drinking.

Because texting combines visual, tactile, and cognitive distraction, it is regarded to be the most hazardous sort of distracted driving. This includes messages. Although drivers between the ages of 16 and 24 have been distracted by technology at larger rates than other drivers since 2007, all drivers are vulnerable to distracted driving incidents. Take notice to these driving safety advice:

If you must text someone, stop your car in a safe spot and park there first.

Assign a "designated texter" to oversee all of your messaging if you are transporting passengers.

Keep your phone in the trunk if you can't resist the impulse to check it.

Consequences of Reckless Driving

What Is Reckless Driving?

Reckless driving is described as operating a vehicle with a purposeful or wanton disregard for the safety of other persons. It is a major offense to drive carelessly in the state of California. If someone breaches any of the following driving restrictions, they may obtain a ticket for reckless driving. going too swiftly. In most places, drivers who exceed the legal speed limit are instantly assessed a reckless driving penalty. These penalties are commonly dished out by state law enforcement officials to drivers who violate the declared speed limit by more than 25 miles per hour. breaching traffic laws. Both drivers who knowingly violate stop signs and established traffic signals as well as those who swerve in and out of lanes may be found guilty of reckless driving.

racing Drivers who are reckless may purposefully choose to race their automobiles on public roadways, putting everyone on the road, including themselves, in significant danger. When drivers try to gain an advantage by taking up both lanes on a two-lane road or by trying to cross into the other lane of traffic, racing becomes exceedingly dangerous.

utilizing a blind curve. Most streets feature a broken yellow line that clearly shows where passing is allowed. When driving on a road with a solid yellow line, drivers need to remain out of each other's path, even if the vehicle in front is traveling too slowly. The chance of an accident can be greatly raised when driving around a blind curve as it may be impossible to spot oncoming cars.
avoiding or circumnavigating railroad obstructions. The function of railroad barriers is to keep automobiles off the train tracks when a train is passing. Drivers who violate these barriers face the danger of being hit by a train; those who do not risk being penalized with reckless driving.

driving by a school bus that has its lights flashing and its stop sign extended. When a school bus flashes its lights and extends its stop sign, it's letting students get on or off the bus. Disregarding this message may significantly damage minors. Reckless driving fines could emerge even for drivers who pass a school bus carefully.

attempting to avoid or flee a law enforcement agent. There are drivers who will stop at nothing to avoid getting stopped by the police. Regrettably, reckless driving may entail things like speeding, swerving, or performing other unlawful activities to get away from a police.

driving whilst inebriated. Reckless driving is more likely among persons who drive a motor vehicle while under the influence of alcohol or drugs. Charges for risky driving may occasionally be brought about merely by the act of driving while inebriated.

driving while preoccupied. Distracted driving is described as participating in any activity that draws your concentration away from the road. These duties, which include texting, reading, and eating, could be cognitive or manual.

reckless driving. When driving, aggressive drivers may choose to show their frustrations or wrath by speeding excessively or cutting other cars off in traffic, among other unsafe and irresponsible driving actions.

Possible Repercussions of Careless Driving

The likelihood of an accident is greatly elevated when driving recklessly. When driving too swiftly, you have to respond substantially quicker and you run the danger of incurring far more injuries in the case of an accident. Not only that, but driving carelessly may result in significant repercussions like fines and citations if it puts the safety of other people or property at danger.

You might be given a ticket and associated sanctions if a police officer catches you driving carelessly, especially if the reckless action causes an accident.cancellation of your license. License suspension may arise from driving extremely irresponsibly or from driving recklessly on several instances. If you continue to drive dangerously, you might in some situations have your license permanently revoked.

increased prices for insurance. Driving recklessly increases your risk of an accident, and your insurance company does not want to pay for it. Therefore, if you are discovered to be driving recklessly, your insurance premiums may increase sometimes drastically. Having problems filling specific posts. If you have a conviction for reckless driving, you might find it difficult to acquire a position where operating a motor vehicle is a frequent need. Additionally, you might find it difficult to secure a position in some government agencies or other places that require a high degree of ethics and trust.

equipping your automobile with an ignition interlock device. Installing an ignition interlock device on a vehicle may be required for intoxicated drivers who drive dangerously. This can result in reduced driving privileges, such as a restricted license that only allows you use it to drive to work or school during specified hours.

Time behind jail. Your irresponsible driving behaviors may put you in jail in certain cases. If an accident resulting in major harm or death was caused by your reckless actions, you might be more likely to go to prison.

Steer wary of reckless driving

It is your job as a motorist to contribute to ensuring the safety of other drivers on the road. Every time you take a vehicle, you contribute to the safety of every other driver and passenger. Do you find it difficult to resist from driving carelessly? Try applying a couple of these strategies.

- Review the traffic restrictions once again. Become more familiar with the California Driver Guide. Make sure you are aware of the average speed limitations in rural and highway zones, when you may safely pass, and any other facts that may impact your ability to drive on Washington state roads.
- Decelerate Every time you drive, take note of the speed limit and create the habit of maintaining at or below it, especially in dangerous conditions. You may need to retrain yourself to obey the speed limit if you have a habit of speeding.
- Give yourself ample time to reach your place. Feeling rushed is a typical cause of reckless driving behavior. You might find it tough to drive safely when you have to hurry to get there. On the other hand, allowing plenty of time could assist you keep away of reckless driving behaviors.
- Observe the road around you. Steer clear of distracted driving and multitasking, and create the habit of paying attention to everything around you. Keep an eye on adjacent traffic patterns and other cars. This may frequently stop you from unwittingly driving aggressively, especially in unexpected locations.

What to Do If a Driver Is Careless

You have authority over how you drive, but you have no impact on how other people drive. Nonetheless, you can reduce the potential damage that reckless drivers could cause to you and your passengers. To help defend oneself from reckless drivers, try these strategies.

- Should You Enter a Vehicle with an Idle Driver
- Draw attention to the acts. Call attention to the problem and recommend that the driver of your automobile stop if you notice them exceeding the speed limit, swerving through traffic, or using a mobile phone while driving. While some drivers may be ready to minimize their reckless driving when prompted by their passengers, many drivers may not be conscious of their own unsafe driving behaviors, especially when they are sleepy or busy.
- Put an end to the ride. If the driver for your Lyft or Uber is behaving abnormally, stop the ride and report the reason on the app. Make sure you submit a review so that other passengers will know not to travel with that exact driver. Inform your companion or loved one that you desire to get out of the automotive when you're in it. To avoid upsetting someone, try not to "wait it out" or "hope for the best." You don't want to incur injuries from irresponsible driving, which may have serious ramifications for you and other passengers in the vehicle.

- If you need help, call for it. Call for help if a negligent driver refuses to stop or let you get out of their vehicle and you find yourself trapped inside. While you wait for the driver to be pulled over, contact 911. For a ride, you don't have to put yourself in risk.
- Avoid conversing to the other motorist. For example, avoid the desire to stop a reckless driver so they can't pass you. Avoid utilizing hand gestures or other motions that can annoy the other driver. A driver who is furious on the road may choose to follow you until you stop or may act in a manner that is considerably more damaging for you and your passengers. Instead, keep as near to the reckless driver as you can while driving normally.
- Please step aside if you can. If necessary, pull over to the side of the road and wait for an irresponsible driver to go by. The probability that a reckless driver may damage you or your passengers will diminish if you step aside. Get your vehicle to a safe spot if you observe a reckless driver growing furious with you. Until help comes or you are convinced that the other driver has moved on, try not to get out of the car.
- Make a 911 call. In the event that you notice consistently reckless driving and feel worried for the safety of other drivers, pull over to a secure spot and either you or a passenger should notify 911. Provide the car's make and model, license plate number, and where you are right now. The careless driver will be stopped by police officers.

How Do Car Accidents Result From Careless Driving?

Driving recklessly may heighten the probability of crashes and lead to more serious injuries when they do occur. After an accident, it could result in more severe repercussions for drivers, such as higher fines or license suspension. But if you are wounded in an accident caused by someone else's irresponsible driving, the other driver's conduct might damage your case dramatically. Think about

Driving recklessly contributes in attributing responsibility for the crash. The motorist may be held more liable for the crash if you are aware that the other vehicle was driving carelessly. However, you may still be deemed partly accountable for the crash if your own negligent actions—such as speeding or running red lights contributed to the collision, which can limit the amount of compensation you obtain.

Consequences of Driving Without a License or Insurance

<u>**What penalties exist in California for driving a car without insurance?**</u>
Every driver in California who uses a car on the road is needed to obtain auto insurance. Driving without insurance may have catastrophic ramifications. Depending on whether it's a first-time or repeat infringement, the penalty may be as high as $500, which includes towing the automobile and suspending the driver's license.

First-Time Offense: You may be penalized between $100 and $200 if you are detected driving without insurance in California for the first time. This cost may also be raised by penalty assessments, which may bring the total after extra fees and assessments to about $450. The impounding of automobiles is an additional possibility.

Recurring Offenses: The fines for a second violation escalate to $200–$500, and penalty assessments may bring this sum to $520–$1,300. More harsher consequences, such as impounding a vehicle and suspending a driver's license for up to four years, may also be applicable, particularly for repeat offenders.
Rising Insurance Premiums: In addition to the immediate penalty, being found driving without insurance in California may result in a considerable hike in your auto insurance premiums when you seek coverage.

<u>**Which California laws are applicable to vehicle insurance?**</u>
Section 16028(a) of the California Vehicle Code requires drivers to carry proof of their financial commitment, which is generally evidence of vehicle insurance. When questioned, drivers must produce this papers to law enforcement.

Section 16020 of the California Vehicle Code demands that all drivers and motor vehicle owners must always be able to show their financial responsibility in line with Section 16021 and carry evidence of the sort of financial responsibility that is in place for their vehicle.

Sections 16020–16033 of the California Vehicle Code: Together, these parts outline the state's laws for car insurance and define the requirements of drivers to maintain proper insurance or other kinds of financial accountability.

Section 11580.1 of the California Insurance Code states: This provision states that unless a policy of car liability insurance fulfills the requirements outlined in provision 16054 of the Vehicle Code, it cannot be issued or delivered in California and will not cover liability resulting from the ownership, maintenance, or use of any motor vehicle.

11580.1b, the California Insurance Code: The state's minimum liability insurance requirements for private passenger automobiles are explained in this section, with a focus on liability coverage for damages to third parties (rather than the policyholder) under a fault-based system.

These rules attempt to assure that Californian drivers and vehicle owners maintain a basic degree of financial responsibility, usually via liability insurance, to pay any losses or injury to third parties in the event of an automobile accident. Respecting these guidelines is vital to keep out of problems with the law and to make sure you have a safety net in case anything goes wrong.

What happens if you don't have insurance and are involved in a vehicle accident in California?

Fines and License Suspension: Following an accident, the state may suspend your driver's license for a year if you are unable to present documentation of vehicle insurance. In addition, there will be a fine enforced. The maximum punishment for a single offense is $200, while the maximum fine for subsequent crimes is $500. If there are extra penalties and costs, you might have to pay a lot more.

Impoundment of Vehicles: You might have to pay for any towing and storage expenses if your automobile is impounded. This is true for both first and repeated offenses.

SR-22 Requirement: You may need to receive an SR-22 form, or a proof of financial responsibility, if you are in an accident. This requirement, which generally lasts three years, acts as a notice to insurers and the DMV that you are a high-risk driver.

Personal Liability for Damages and Medical Expenses: In the event that the accident results in damages and medical expenses, you may be held personally accountable if you do not have insurance. This suggests that you might have to pay for these charges out of pocket.

Recovering Non-Economic Damages is Limited: Even in circumstances where you are not at fault for the accident, you may not be able to claim non-economic damages like pain and suffering if you are uninsured and get into an accident in California. This legislation does have some limitations, however, such as if the at-fault driver was incapacitated by alcohol or drugs when the incident happened.

citation for Driving Without Enough Insurance: You may still obtain a citation for driving without insurance even if you are not at fault in the incident. When additional penalties and charges are taken into consideration, the punishment for this infringement may be fairly expensive.

In the event that a Californian motorist hits me without insurance, what should I do?

There are a few things you should do in California if someone strikes you without insurance in order to handle the case professionally:

- First, make sure that everyone who was a part of the incident is safe. If necessary, move to a safe spot, and notify emergency services if someone is wounded.
- **Speak with the police:** Inform the police about the accident. Particularly when dealing with an uninsured driver, a police record is crucial. It provides as an official record of the occurrence and may be important for legal and insurance claims.
- **Information Sharing**: With the other driver, exchange contact and automobile data. Obtaining the other driver's contact information is vital, even when they do not have insurance.
- **Record the Situation**: Take images of the crash location that illustrate the damage to the two automobiles as well as any important road conditions or signs. Taking images of the event could aid you with your insurance claim and any subsequent legal procedures.
- **Inform Your Insurance Provider**: Report the accident to your insurance carrier as soon as you can. Your uninsured motorist coverage may aid in compensating for damages and injuries brought on by an uninsured driver.
- **Uninsured Motorist Coverage**: Your automobile insurance policy's uninsured motorist coverage may pay for bodily injury and property damage brought on by an uninsured driver. To learn about the processes and coverage limits, consult your policy or chat with your insurance provider.
- **Seek Medical Attention**: Get medical care straight once if you or your passengers are wounded. Seeing a medical specialist is vital as some injuries may not be recognized immediately away.
- **Maintain Documents**: All accident-related data, such as medical bills, repair estimates, and communication with your insurance provider, should be maintained on file.

- **Think About Legal Advice**: If there are serious injuries or differences about who is at responsibility, you may want to consult with an attorney, depending on the degree of the accident and the damages experienced.
- **Subsequent Action:** Maintain touch with your insurance provider and follow to their recommendations on the filing of claims. Follow the progress of the claim and submit any extra facts that may be required.

Recall that it is against the law to drive in California without insurance, making dealing with an uninsured driver more challenging. Your next steps will be dictated by your insurance coverage as well as the particulars of the occurrence

Chapter 7: Licensing and Vehicle Registration

Application Process for Driver's License

A California driver's license (DL) is a document that permits you to drive a car. Your true entire name, birthdate, postal address, signature, photo, and physical description are all provided on a DL. Every time you drive a vehicle, you have to have the card on you.

Types of Licenses DLs come into two basic categories: **noncommercial** and **commercial**. There are license subcategories within the noncommercial category that enable drivers to operate various kinds of motor vehicles.

Four types of noncommercial DLs exist

Fundamental DL (Class C): A common automobile or truck suitable for individual use on California highways. Possessing a Class C driver's license permits you to tow: a lone automobile that weighs no more than 10,000 pounds gross weight (GVWR) (with a tow dolly).
When a vehicle is unloaded and weighs at least 4,000 pounds, a Travel trailer or fifth-wheel coach under 10,000 pounds. GVWR in cases where towing is done for free.
a fifth-wheel travel trailer that weights more than 10,000 but less than 15,000 pounds. GVWR, with endorsement, and in non-compensated towing scenarios.
Motorcycles are two-wheeled motorized vehicles **(Class M1 or M2)**. See how to submit a motorcycle license application.
Fifth wheel/travel trailer **(Noncommercial Class A):** greater than 15,000 pounds gross vehicle weight rating (GVWR) or, in the case that the towing is done without charge, more than 10,000 pounds GVWR for a trailer coach.
Noncommercial Class B housecar/motorhome: 40 feet or more, but not more than 45 feet (with endorsement).

How to File an Application for a Driver's License (DL)

if You're Not Yet Eighteen
You may take your driving test after meeting the terms of your temporary instruction permit. You have to:
- be in the age range of 16 to 18.

- have at least six months' worth of experience holding your temporary teaching permit.
- having accomplished their driving instruction.
- own six hours of expert driving training under their belt.
- hold a valid California driver's license and have completed 50 hours of practice with an adult 25 years of age or older who can testify to your completion of the requisite 50 hours.
- Of the fifty practice hours, at least 10 should be spent practicing night driving.

To go for your driving test

Make an appointment for a driving test (you cannot take a driving test without one). To arrange an appointment, you may also give 1-800-777-0133 a call during regular business hours.

Present proof of financial responsibility (insurance) that fulfills or exceeds the insurance rules in California.

If you don't pass your driving test, you won't be allowed to repeat it for 14 days (not including the day you failed). A retesting fee of $7 is applied. Your application is invalid and you have to reapply if you fail the driving test three times.

Until your new driver's license comes in the mail, the DMV will grant you a temporary license after you pass the driving test. The 60-day temporary DL is in effect. Your DL will come in the mail in three to four weeks. After 60 days, call 1-800-777-0133 to check out the status if you still haven't acquired your new driver's license.

NOTE: You may drive in California for a maximum of 10 days if you are 16 or 17 years old and hold a valid driver's license from another country. If you acquire a nonresident minor's certificate from the DMV, you are authorized to drive for longer than ten days.

You have given the DMV with documentation of your financial accountability.

When driving, you must have your driver's license, proof of financial responsibility, and nonresident minor's certificate in your immediate possession.

Methods for Obtaining a Driver's License (DL)

if You're Older Than Eighteen

To drive an automobile, every resident of California must have a valid California driver's license. The prerequisites for your application may fluctuate based on your circumstances (see below).

First scenario: "I've never had a DL."
- Until your time to take your driving test arrives, you may receive an instruction permit if you are over eighteen and have never held a driver's license in any state or country.
- For drivers under the age of eighteen, merely a temporary instruction permit is necessary. Anyone over the age of 18 would be awarded an instruction permit.
- You may take the driving test to earn a California driver's license (DL) after completing the terms of the instruction permit.

second scenario: "I have a DL issued by another state,"
- If you presently hold a valid driver's license from another state, you may apply for a California driver's license as follows:
- Fill out an application for a driver's license or identification card (DL/ID).
- When you go to a DMV office, you will:Give your SSN (social security number).
- Present a valid identification document (original or certified copy) to confirm your identity for a DL/ID card that conforms with REAL ID regulations or is Federal Non-Compliant. The name on the identity document and your current name must match (for additional information, check the FAQs below).
- Show proper evidence of residency if you do not presently hold a California driver's license or identification.
- Refundable application costs must be paid; the application and cost are valid for a year.
- Get a scan of your thumbprint.
- ace the eye exam.
- Take a photo of yourself.
- Pass the test(s) of knowledge. To pass all of the requisite knowledge tests, you have three opportunities. You will have to reapply if you fail the same test three times, at which point your application becomes invalid. We don't deliver knowledge examinations within 30 minutes after closing in order to allow ample time for assessment.

Third scenario:"I have a DL issued by another country,"

- Use the application method for "I have a DL issued by another state" indicated above if your driver's license was issued by a foreign country.
- To receive an original California driver's license, you will also need to pass a driving test.

To go for your driving test

- Make an appointment for a driving test (you cannot take a driving test without one).
- Present proof of financial responsibility (insurance) that fulfills or exceeds the insurance rules in California.

TAKE NOTE

An accompanying driver is essential to and from the driving test if you hold a valid driver's license from another country You are given three opportunities to pass the driving test using the application fee you paid. In the case that you do not pass the driving exam, you will need to reschedule on a different day and pay the $7 retest penalty. Your application is invalid and you have to reapply if you fail the driving test three times.

Fourth scenario: "I can prove my legal presence in California, but I am not eligible for a DL."

- A conventional or REAL ID driving license or identification (DL/ID) card may be provided to any Californian who can establish their current legal presence in the United States (U.S.) using one of the accepted identity documents (original or certified copy). This covers all citizens of the United States, permanent residents who are not citizens of the United States (Green Card holders), and anyone with temporary legal status, such as those who are eligible for Temporary Protected Status (TPS) or Deferred Action for Childhood Arrivals (DACA), as well as people who have a valid work or study visa. Depending on their immigration status, Californians with temporary legal status may get a new card with a verified extension of their legal status, although their present DL/ID card expires on the same date as their U.S. legal presence certificate.
- For a DL/ID card that is REAL ID compliant or Federal Non-Compliant, check the entire list of acceptable identity documents.

There are various other options to show your legitimate presence in the US:

- You may offer a U.S. birth certificate, passport, or passport card if you were born here.
- You may offer a Permanent Resident Card or a document verifying your naturalization or citizenship if you are an immigrant to the nation.

- You may display a Temporary Resident Identification card or other temporary resident documents if you are not an immigrant but are authorized to stay in the country.

Procedure for Applications

- If you have never made an online account with the DMV before, be ready to do so. If so, be ready to access your DMV online account. (DMV implements two-factor authentication, which requires an email address and a way to receive text messages or phone calls, to validate your digital identity.)
- Along with your name, address, and birthday, make sure you have your social security number on accessible.
- This application takes roughly nine minutes to complete on average. After 15 minutes, the app times out for security and privacy reasons. Don't worry if you can't complete the application in one sitting; you can finish it later by entering into your DMV account. (Applications are only handled when you visit a DMV field office; they are retained for up to a year.)
- You will need to visit a field office to complete the remaining phases of the driver's license/ID card application process after completing the application.

Understanding Vehicle Registration Requirements

Is your automobile registered in California?

As easy as you may think! Even better, you may complete your registration application online.

1. Present a title as evidence of possession

Prior to registering the car in the state of California, you will need to present evidence of ownership. Verify that your name appears on the title or that it has been transferred to your name. If you are transferring ownership, preserve the bill of sale; the DMV will require it for car registration.

2. Get Auto Insurance

Make sure you complete this step if you don't have insurance. The following insurance firms offer vehicle insurance:

Almost all vehicle insurance coverage are fairly flexible. Plans that merely offer liability coverage may start as low as $40.

3. Verify that your DMV record is current

If you have any open citations or fines for your automobile, it might delay the registration of your vehicle. If you possess these goods in the state of California, your registration can be revoked.

4. Give These Records In California, When Registering Your Vehicle
- You may register your car in California in person, over the phone, by mail, or online. The following are the relevant documents:
- You Will Need These Things to Register for the First Time:
- The driver's license or identification card issued by your state
- Details of your insurance for the state in which the automobile will be driven
- A payment of sales tax
- The title of your car Records attesting to your car's compliance with safety and emissions regulations
- The registration application for the car
- Private Transaction Or Ownership Transfer:
- Title beneath your name
- Make sure that the "transferred to" line on the title contains the names of all the owners when you transfer an automobile to a new owner. The "assignment of ownership" paragraph on the back of the title needs to be signed by the sellers.
- Bill of Sale and Odometer Disclosure Statement
- Is It Time to Renew Your Car's License? Ensure that you possess these:
- The Vehicle Identification Number (VIN) that you possess
- Number on the driver's license
- Evidence of coverage Number on the license plate
- Evidence of a past registration for your vehicle (registration card)
- Dealer From Out of State? Additionally, bring these:
- Bring the Title of the Manufacturer's Certificate of Origin
- Bill of Sale and Odometer Disclosure Statement

5. Inspection of Smog
- Every automobile in California needs to have its smog tested, with the following exceptions:
- Any gasoline-powered vehicle (including motorcycles and trailers) must be 1975 or older.
- A 1997 and older model OR with a gross vehicle weight exceeding 14,000 pounds is a diesel-powered vehicle.
- It weighs more than 14,000 pounds in weight and is fueled by natural gas.
- an electric car. fewer than eight model years old and fuel-powered.

6. Complete the Auto Registration Form for California.

- Completing the registration form is the final step. Your driver's license number, license plate number, and VIN are necessary.
- You will need to supply the vehicle's accident history as well as any customized tune-ups that have changed how the car drives.
- To find out what expenses apply to your specific automobile, check the California DMV website.
- In California, you have the choice of online or in-person registration.
- In California, you must register your car once a year.

Renewal Procedures and Registration Stickers

- Make sure your address is current before you continue. Change your address if required, but do so no later than three days before commencing the renewal application.
- Prior to commencing, validate that you have The number on your license plate.
- the final five digits of your boat's or vessel's hull identification number (HIN), or vehicle identification number (VIN).
- a message of renewal validating your current postal address.
- Details about your payment.
- There is an additional 1.95% processing fee for credit and debit card transactions.
- If you wish to pay directly out of your bank account, there are no additional expenses.

This is exclusively for renewing your registration as a handicapped person. Separate renewals apply to placards and parking plates.

FAQS FOR REGISTRATION RENEWAL!

Is it feasible for me to amend my registration online?

- If you have access to the Internet, you may renew your registration online.
- You hold a valid bank account, debit card, or credit card.
- You are aware of the final five digits of your automobile or vessel's Hull Identification Number (HIN) or Vehicle Identification Number (VIN).
- Either your automobile is insured, OR you are registering a car (like a trailer) that doesn't require insurance.

- Your car's electronic smog certification data is stored on file with the DMV.
- If you don't, you won't be able to renew your registration online: possess a bank account, credit card, or debit card.
- Find out the VIN or HIN for your automobile.

Online payments are acceptable for automobile registration charges; however, if a vehicle still requires an insurance certificate or a smog certificate, registration is not complete.

I'm signing in to renew my registration. Does the browser I'm using matter?

I propose using one of these web browsers in its most current version:

- Chrome by Google
- Microsoft Edge
- Firefox on Mozilla
- Safari (OS X/iOS)

For the DMV website to load effectively, JavaScript needs to be enabled in your browser.

Try a different browser from the list above if you are encountering troubles with the one you are presently using. In the event that your troubles continue,

How long will it take for me to acquire my updated registration and registration sticker in the mail if I renew online?

- Within two weeks, you will receive a letter with your new registration and sticker.
- To obtain an idea of how long it will take for your registration to arrive in the mail, you may also visit the Vehicle Registration Renewals website for current processing timelines.

In the case that my address changes, may I renew online?

- You surely can. Before trying to renew your registration online, you must first make an online address modification.
- Waiting three business days between altering your address online and renewing your registration will enable the system to update your information and guarantee that your new registration is issued to your revised address.

I would wish to send in my registration renewal. Is that acceptable?

- The majority of customers may renew online. Even better, you may pay with a card or check and retain the stamp!

- Additionally, you may save a stamp by renewing over the phone by giving a call at 1-800-777-0133.
- Additionally, if you have the time to wait and need to renew by mail, send to:

- PO Box 942897 Sacramento, CA 94269-0001 DMV Renewal

What is keeping everyone from renewing their registration online?
- An insurance card is one of the documentation that you may occasionally need to give to the DMV. In such circumstance, you are unable to renew online because the DMV wants that information to be on file in order to process your online renewal.

I would wish to renew my online registration. Does the insurance provider I select matter?

Indeed. Only if your insurance provider electronically provides data to DMV are you eligible to renew online.

This year, I'm not going to drive my automobile. Does the renewal fee still need to be paid?
- No. You must submit an online application for Planned Nonoperation if you wish to store your automobile rather than use it this year. The PNO filing fee will then need to be paid.
- If you choose to drive your car or park it somewhere where it may acquire a parking ticket after filing for PNO, you will be liable for paying the complete year's worth of vehicle registration fees and penalties.

What happens if my parking fees have already been paid?
- Prior to renewing your registration online, all parking penalties must be paid or cleared.
- Should those parking fines still be included on the DMV renewal letter you receive, you should mail or visit a DMV shop to finalize the renewal procedure.
- You must resolve your parking ticket disagreement with the court if you wish to oppose it. Once the court has dismissed your parking ticket, mail or visit a DMV shop to turn in your clearance form and renewal notice.

A few weeks ago, I filed my renewal fees, but my check hasn't processed yet. How should I proceed?

- Do not set a stop payment on your check if you have paid your renewal expenses but it hasn't cleared. It's possible that the department is still processing your payment.
- If your check hasn't cleared after eight weeks of renewing your registration, contact the DMV at 1-800-777-0133.

My car's smog certification was refused even though I made my registration payments, and I still haven't paid my parking fees. Does my registration stay active?

- Your registration will not be renewed even if you make the registration fees if your automobile does not meet additional requirements (such as smog certification or unpaid parking penalties). In this situation, renewing your registration is dependant upon paying your parking penalties or receiving your smog certification.

What measures should I take if my automobile will stay registered in California even if I'm migrating out of state?

- Within ten days of your relocation, you must inform the DMV of your address change.
- To advise the DMV of a change of home or postal address for the records of your vehicle, boat, driver's license, or identification card, you may do so online.

I don't have a driver's license and I'm underage. Is it feasible to register an automobile now?

- No, it is prohibited for any adolescent to order, acquire, lease, or receive an automobile as a gift if they do not yet hold a valid driver's license.

How Can I Replace Stickers or Certificates That Are Lost, Stolen, or Mutilated?

- You may submit an Application for Replacement or Transfer of Title (REG 227), pay a duplicate fee, and report your stolen or damaged California Certificate of Ownership.
- You may replace lost certificates and/or stickers combined with the appropriate money by completing a completed Application for Replacement Plates, Stickers, Documents (REG 156) if you lose the registration card or sticker.
- These forms may be delivered to the DMV by mail or handed in in person at a DMV facility.

Interacting with the DMV for License and Registration Services

It could be challenging to navigate the Department of Motor Vehicles (DMV) when seeking license and registration services, but you can make the process move more quickly if you're prepared and have some knowledge. Obtaining the needed papers, including identity, proof of residency, and social security number, is the first step in commencing the license application process. If at all practicable, arrange an online appointment to avoid waiting.

When you get there, bring patience. DMV offices generally see a lot of traffic, and lengthy lineups are not unusual. Deliver your documentation, pay any fees that are required, and take any exams or examinations that are needed. Make sure you have the title to your automobile, documentation of insurance, and other relevant papers before registering it.

Keep in mind that every state might have different requirements, so it's wise to find out the actual guidelines that apply to your location. The DMV's online tools and FAQs may supply useful information. When you can, utilize their online services to avoid waiting in person and save time.

Dealing with the DMV doesn't have to be a bother; it's merely a formal procedure to assure traffic safety and adherence to laws. You'll soon have your license and registration in hand and be prepared to hit the wide road if you stay informed and have patience.

Chapter 8: Additional Resources and Contacts

Important Contact Information for DMV Offices

- Make sure you have access to your driver's license, identification card, license plate number, and vehicle identifying number (VIN).
- Internet-Based Services
- Visit dmv.ca.gov/vrservices to renew your vehicle's registration.
- Visit dmv.ca.gov/dlservices for driver's license renewal, and dmv.ca.gov/make-an-appointment for office appointments.
- Find many more online services at dmv.ca.gov/online.
- Kiosk Services
- For information on kiosk locations and services, go to dmv.ca.gov/kiosks.
- Telephone Services Dial 1-800-777-0133.
- In the course of normal business hours: Speak with a DMV staff.
- 24/7 Autonomous Phone Services:
- Renew the registration on your automobile.
- Schedule a time at the DMV office.
- For support, persons who are hard of hearing, deaf, or have speech problems may call 1-800-368-4327.

Useful Online Resources for California Drivers

The top five tools to help you ace your DMV test are mentioned below.

1. No-cost DMV practice test

You may prepare for the real thing by taking one of the numerous free DMV practice examinations that are given online. Because our DMV practice examinations are almost comparable to the actual test you will take at the DMV, this is the perfect technique to prepare ready.

2. The Handbook for Drivers

Every state has a driver's handbook that covers all of the state's traffic rules and regulations. You should learn everything in this manual in your driver's ed class, but before the practice test, make sure you read everything on your own.

Try reading it in pieces, and after each one, give yourself a test. Take note of all the traffic signs and their meanings. If necessary, prepare flashcards and go over the most tough portions more than once. recollection that this is not simply for recollection. After you pass your test, you will be able to drive every day with the use of this information.

3. Grownup Drivers

It's probable that you have some adult pals who are now and have been drivers for some time. Thus, submit queries to them! See if they can aid if you need clarification on a specific topic. Alternatively, ask them to help you in constructing a practice test. It's conceivable that they will reveal some extra information.

And when you're being chauffeured around by an adult, ask questions. To develop as a driver, you could interrogate them about the logic behind their judgments while they're driving. Having supportive persons in your life who have gone through the same thing as you helps relieve your nervousness and get you ready for the DMV test.

4. Actual Traffic Signs

Now is the time to put the knowledge you gained from your driver's handbook to work in real driving circumstances. Always pay great attention to your surroundings whether you are driving a vehicle or simply riding about.

Examine every sign that you saw on a DMV practice test or that you read about in the manual to see how it functions in the real world. In order to assist you imagine them later on during the test, attempt to commit them to memory. Having a practical experience with a subject you learnt often makes it easier to recall.

5. Healthful Routines

As with any test, you should prepare for the examination by exercising excellent habits. This will help you perform well on it. Make sure you had a full night's sleep the night before and start your day with a healthy, well-balanced lunch.

Before your test, you may desire to participate in some modest activity to enhance blood flow and alleviate any nervousness you may be experiencing.

Try to arrange your test appointment in the morning if at all practicable. In this way, you may complete it and minimize any test-related stress you might be having.

Don't get too worked up about failing the DMV test the first time. Ultimately, one of the finest pieces of counsel we've ever heard is to "try, try again!" However, if you make use of these resources, you'll undoubtedly ace your DMV permit test!

Applications

MOBILIO: The program records driving behavior and rewards careful drivers.
ReadItToMe: The programs read users' incoming text messages aloud.
RoadReady: This program supports youngsters in monitoring their driving growth and learning   safe driving skills.
SAFE 2 SAVE: With its reward structure, the app promotes safe driving practices.

Additional Study Tips and Test-Taking Strategies

Improving your test-taking techniques and study habits may make a big difference in your academic performance. To maximize your educational experience, take into account the following extra advice:

1. Test your knowledge of the subject matter to participate in active recall. This might be teaching the material to someone else, making flashcards, or summarizing the important ideas. Your memory becomes stronger when you actively retrieve knowledge.

2. Make a variety of study materials. To get a thorough grasp of the topic, combine lecture notes, videos, textbooks, and internet resources. Various formats may provide a range of viewpoints, which can strengthen your understanding of the material.

3. Plan frequent breaks in between study periods. The Pomodoro Technique helps improve attention and reduce burnout. It consists of 25-minute intense study sessions interspersed with 5-minute breaks.

4. Use mind maps to bring difficult ideas to life visually. Creating spatial connections between concepts may help clarify the connections between various topical aspects.

5. Work along with classmates during study sessions. You may reinforce your grasp of topics by explaining them to others, and you can get new insights from debates. Maintain a concentrated atmosphere to increase output.

6. Practice in a setting similar to an exam. Take notes during practice exams, follow the same guidelines as the real exam, and put an end to outside distractions. This enhances time management and reduces exam anxiety.

7. Preserve a sound equilibrium. Make sure you get enough rest, move often, and eat a balanced diet. Mental clarity is influenced by physical health, which improves concentration during study sessions and tests.

8. Examine prior materials on a regular basis. Analyze your learning progress and note any areas that need further practice. Long-term retention is aided by regular evaluation.

9. Never be afraid to ask for assistance when you need it. Seeking clarification on difficult subjects from academic resources, students, or instructors might help stop misconceptions from becoming worse.

10. Envision yourself triumphant. During the test, picture yourself responding to questions with assurance. Confidence and anxiety may be increased with the use of positive imagination.

By incorporating these test-taking techniques and study aids into your daily routine, you may improve your academic performance and overall learning experience.

Sample Road Trip Itineraries and Scenic Routes

The broad expanse of highways and roads opens out in front of you, signaling an experience full of pace, precision, and the continuous pounding of tires on pavement. Every lane and junction becomes a note in the huge composition of your drive as you move into the highway symphony.

1. The expressway sonata may be accessible via the entry ramp, which acts as a precursor to velocity. As you easily move into the flow, you'll feel the acceleration—a taste of the pace that's to come.

2. The harmony in motion is specified by the lanes, which are akin to musical staves on sheet music. Drive with precision, picking the proper lane for your pace, and easing into and out of traffic as the highway regulates the flow.

3. merge points: spots where automobiles play together like a band. Find your space in the traffic symphony, announce your intentions, and coordinate your actions.

4. Overtaking, a crescendo that accelerates. Determine the pace of incoming traffic, move smoothly, and fade into the background like a fleeting note in a song.

5. Conversations, the musical transitions on your road. As you make your way through the complicated passages and elegantly transition from one action to the next, follow the suggestions.

6. The magnificent breaks and wayside views that are part of the route composition. Observe the moving environment, which incorporates both rural and metropolis skylines, each of which extends a different movement within the symphony.

7. ramps for departure, a descending movement when you are ready to go. Give notice of your purpose, ease off the highway ramp, and turn into local streets.

8. Relaxation areas are pleasant pauses along the route. Before going on to the next movement, take a time to recharge and allow the symphony to breathe.

9. Traffic flow, a synchronized ensemble. Be conscious of other passengers' behavior and maintain a group cadence to assure a tranquil and enjoyable ride.

10. The glorious culmination of the highway symphony is your arrival. Drive the remaining few kilometers with precision, finishing your vehicle song elegantly when you reach your destination.

You are the conductor and composer while driving on freeways and highways, organizing your car across the various lanes, crossroads, and gorgeous portions. Every movement of the highway symphony becomes a chapter in the enthralling drama of your voyage, giving it a memorable and musical experience while you drive.

Conclusion

In concluding this California DMV Handbook 2024, I extend my sincere gratitude to you, the reader, for choosing this guide as your companion on the journey to becoming a proficient and responsible driver in the Golden State. Your commitment to mastering the intricacies of California's roadways is commendable, and I trust that the knowledge gained from these pages will empower you for years to come.

Throughout this handbook, we've embarked on a comprehensive exploration of the rules, regulations, and nuances that define California's driving landscape. From decoding traffic signs to navigating complex intersections, each chapter is a carefully curated piece of the puzzle, designed to enhance your understanding and proficiency as a driver.

As you close these pages, envision yourself not just as someone who has aced the DMV test but as a vigilant and informed driver equipped with the knowledge to navigate the dynamic and diverse roads of California confidently.

Remember, this handbook isn't just about passing a test; it's a key to unlocking the artistry of driving in one of the most scenic and diverse states in the U.S. May your journeys be safe, enjoyable, and filled with the freedom that comes from mastering the rules of the road.

Once again, thank you for choosing the California DMV Handbook 2024. Your commitment to responsible driving contributes to safer roads and a more enjoyable driving experience for all. Wishing you endless miles of safe and memorable travels.

Best wishes for a successful Exam day

Dear Valued Readers,
As you stand on the brink of your upcoming exam, I want to take a moment to extend my heartfelt best wishes to each and every one of you. This journey you've embarked upon, whether it be academic, professional, or personal, reflects your dedication, perseverance, and the relentless pursuit of knowledge and success.

I hope you walk into the test room with self-assurance, a clear head, and an unwavering spirit. You have come this far because to your dedication and hard work, and I am sure you are more than capable of handling the challenges that lie ahead.

Keep in mind that this is a celebration of your growth and perseverance as much as a test of your knowledge. Accept the chance to demonstrate your abilities and recognize that each question is an opportunity to shine.

Put your confidence in yourself and your preparedness to use when faced with uncertainty. You've studied for hours on end, dealt with difficulties, and overcome barriers. It's time to show off your intelligence now.

May you have clarity of thought, unshakable focus, and success in your endeavors. As much as I believe in you, have faith in yourself. Success is a manifestation of your perseverance and commitment, not just a result.

So here's to your success: may you confidently write your responses, skillfully handle obstacles, and proudly finish this journey. Recall that every question presents an opportunity for you to demonstrate your expertise, and every obstacle serves as a step toward your objectives.

Wishing you a brilliantly successful exam. You've got this!

Warm regards,

[Steven J. Wilkins]

Appendix

Congratulations on completing the California DMV Handbook 2024! This appendix is designed to be your gateway to additional resources that will further enrich your understanding of driving in California and empower you as a responsible and informed driver. Explore these valuable materials to enhance your knowledge and stay updated on any changes in driving regulations.

1. DMV Online Services

Access the official California DMV website for the latest updates, forms, and online services. Stay informed about any changes in regulations and access additional resources.

2. Driver's Education Courses

Consider enrolling in a recognized driver's education course. These programs often provide interactive learning experiences, practice tests, and additional insights that complement the information in this handbook.

3. Local DMV Offices

Visit your local DMV office for in-person assistance and to obtain any specific information related to your region. DMV offices are valuable resources for personalized guidance.

4. Traffic Schools

Explore accredited traffic schools that offer courses to enhance your driving skills. These schools often provide valuable insights into defensive driving techniques and safety practices.

5. California Vehicle Code

Delve into the California Vehicle Code for a comprehensive understanding of the laws governing driving in the state. This legal document serves as a detailed reference for various driving regulations.

6. Official California Driver Handbook

For more specifics and information that might enhance the information in this handbook, consult the official California Driver Handbook. Keep abreast on any updates or additions.

7. Online Practice Tests

Engage in online practice tests to reinforce your knowledge and prepare for the DMV written exam. These resources offer a simulated testing environment to build confidence.

8. Community Forums and Groups

Join online forums or community groups where fellow drivers share experiences, advice, and tips. Engaging with a community of drivers can provide valuable insights beyond the content of this handbook.

9. Driving Simulation Apps

　　　

Explore driving simulation apps that allow you to practice various driving scenarios in a virtual environment. These apps can be effective tools for honing your skills.

10. Road Safety Organizations

Connect with reputable road safety organizations for valuable insights and updates on safe driving practices. These organizations often provide educational materials and resources.

Remember, the journey to becoming a skilled and responsible driver is ongoing. Use these resources to continue honing your understanding of California's roadways and ensuring that you stay well-informed throughout your driving adventures. Safe travels!